BRIDGES

BRIDGES

by Scott Corbett · illustrated by Richard Rosenblum

FOUR WINDS PRESS · NEW YORK

LIBRARY OF CONGRESS CATALOGING IN PUBLICATION DATA

Corbett, Scott.
   Bridges.

   Includes index.
   SUMMARY: Discusses the history of bridges from ancient
times to the present and describes the building of various
types of bridges.
   1. Bridges—History—Juvenile literature.
[1. Bridges—History] I. Title.
TG15.C67   624.2′09   77–13871
ISBN 0–590–07464–4

PUBLISHED BY FOUR WINDS PRESS
A DIVISION OF SCHOLASTIC MAGAZINES, INC., NEW YORK, N.Y.
TEXT COPYRIGHT © 1978 BY SCOTT CORBETT
ILLUSTRATIONS COPYRIGHT © 1978 BY RICHARD ROSENBLUM
ALL RIGHTS RESERVED
PRINTED IN THE UNITED STATES OF AMERICA
LIBRARY OF CONGRESS CATALOG CARD NUMBER: 77–13871
2 3 4 5   82 81 80 79

Contents

1 · Bridges Came Before Houses · 1

2 · The First Great Bridge-Builders · 8

3 · When London Bridge Was Built · 23

4 · Renaissance Bridges · 32

5 · The Last Great Stone-Arch Bridges · 40

6 · Bridges, Yankee Style · 48

7 · Iron Horses and Iron Bridges · 55

8 · "The Bridge Is Down!" · 66

9 · Across the Niagara . . . · 78

10 · Across the Mississippi · 84

11 · Brooklyn Bridge · 94

12 · Twentieth-Century Bridges · 104

13 · The Infinite Variety of Bridges · 116

· Index · 120

1

Bridges Came Before Houses

Somewhere in the world there may be people who have never crossed a bridge. There may be some in the Sahara Desert, for instance. Such people are, however, exceedingly rare. For most of us, bridges are a part of life.

Traveling familiar routes in our family cars we grow so accustomed to crossing small bridges and viaducts that we forget they are there. We have to stop and think to remember how often they come along. Only when a bridge is closed for repairs and we have to take a long detour do we realize how difficult life would be without it.

Try to imagine our world with all the bridges removed. In many places life would be seriously disrupted, traffic would be paralyzed, and business would be terrible.

Bridges bring us together and keep us together. They are a basic necessity for civilization.

The first structures human beings built were bridges. Before prehistoric people began to build even the crudest shelter for themselves, they bridged streams. Early prehistoric tribes were wanderers. Since they did not stay in one place they did not think of building themselves

1

houses. But they could not wander far without finding a stream in their way.

Nature provided the first bridges. Finding themselves confronted with some narrow but rapid river, humans noticed a tree that had fallen across the river from bank to bank. The person who first scrambled across a fallen log, perhaps after watching monkeys run across it, was the first human being to cross a bridge.

Eventually, when they had learned how to chop down a tree, they also learned how to make a tree fall in the direction they wanted it to fall. The wandering tribe that first deliberately made a tree fall across a stream were the first bridge-builders.

In the meantime, in jungle areas, other tribes were beginning to use another kind of bridge.

Wherever vines happened to reach from the trees on one bank of a stream to trees on the other side, we may be sure that monkeys swung across on them. Sooner or later someone watched them and decided to try the trick himself. Trial and error—a few falls when the vine broke under his weight and tumbled him into the stream—gave him the idea of making stronger cables out of several vines.

But stronger vine cables would mean larger cables, which would be harder to grip. Perhaps two parallel cables, one to grip with each hand, were the next improvement. Then came the idea of connecting these parallel cables with some sort of crosspieces, so that people could crawl across.

Soon someone—teenage daredevils, probably—tried to walk across. After a few of them had fallen off into the river, some early safety engineer must have thought of adding two more cables above the others, to provide hand-grips while crossing; and to this day primitive suspension bridges of this four-cable variety are still being used in many parts of the world. Often the space between the top and bottom cable on each side is filled in with vertical suspenders, providing greater strength and safety.

A different kind of thrill was provided by suspension bridges built in northeast India. There single bamboo poles were stretched across chasms above streams. A traveler would fit a loop of bamboo over one end of the pole and sit in the loop. His weight would cause the pole to sag. Down its length he would slide, faster and faster, and partway up the other slope of the pole. When he slowed down he had to catch hold of the pole and pull himself hand over hand the rest of the way.

Some of the most spectacular primitive suspension bridges were built in the highlands of Peru, where turbulent rivers cutting through deep canyons made migrations impossible for Indian tribes without the help of bridges.

One such bridge, spanning a chasm 148 feet wide, swung 118 feet above the Apurimac River. How was a bridge that long ever constructed at such a height? First, some of the more daring young warriors had to climb down to the river, get across the best way they could, and climb up the far side of the canyon. Next, one of the chieftains ordered a good bowman to shoot an arrow across the canyon, an arrow with a long thread tied to it.

Once the thread had reached the warriors on the far bank, a stronger cord was attached to it and pulled across. Thicker ropes could now be carried back and forth until several thicknesses could be bundled together into two cables of sufficient strength to support the weight of

PERUVIAN SUSPENSION BRIDGE

not only the men, women, and children of the tribe but their pack animals as well. Branches and saplings laid close together across the cables and lashed to them with strips of leather or hemp provided the footwalk.

Suspension bridges were a natural development in warm climates where there were plenty of strong vines or long, straight bamboo poles. In other places, however, the problem was more often one of crossing a wide river with low banks. In these places the pier bridge was developed.

There are many rivers and streams that are too wide to be spanned by a single log. Sometimes there was a small island or a pile of rocks out in the center of the stream and this probably led to the idea of building up the rock piles sufficiently to use them as a midway support for two or more logs. If there were more trees than rocks available as building materials, a wickerwork of branches or saplings was constructed and placed out in the stream to serve as a pier. Eventually, to make these piers stronger, someone got the idea of filling the wickerwork with small rocks.

In the Swiss lake district during the Bronze Age prehistoric people known as the lake dwellers were the first to construct bridges on piles. Their piles were logs which they drove into the mud of the lake bottom. This must have been extremely difficult work to do with primitive tools; but somehow they managed to drive the piles deep enough to provide steady uprights on which to build a footwalk to their huts, which were also built on pilings out over the water.

Early bridges were always built of material that was close at hand. In tropical jungle areas, where vines were plentiful, primitive suspension bridges resulted. In forested areas wood was used. In northern areas the Ice Age had left its mark. Glaciers had wiped out the forests and left behind a landscape littered with rocks, boulders, shale, and gravel. Here, as elsewhere, bridges were made of material that was available. Piers built of stones were connected by thin slabs of flat stone.

Sometime in the very distant past, in China, another basic bridge form was developed—the cantilever bridge. A cantilever is a balanced structure extending out diagonally on both sides of a pier. Two of these sections can either meet in the middle or approach closely enough to support a center span. The cantilever principle can also be used, for instance, by driving poles diagonally into both banks of a river so that they extend upward and outward to provide support for the platform of a bridge.

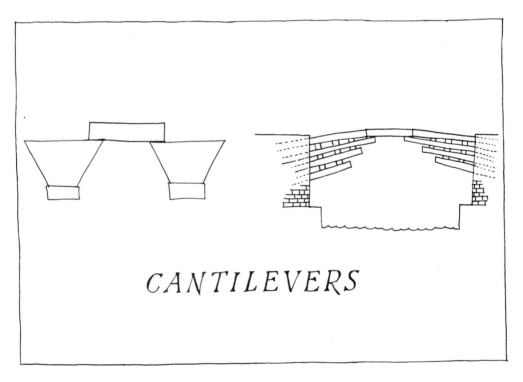

CANTILEVERS

From the beginning, the idea of building bridges must have appealed to people not only as a necessity but as a challenge—few structures we have built involve as much danger. The place where a bridge is to be built is seldom an easy one to work in; if it were, there would probably be no need for a bridge.

Bridges are a direct challenge to nature, however, and that fact has often made people uneasy. Early man believed that every river was ruled by its own gods who would resent the spanning of their river by a bridge. Before the coming of a bridge, people would have been crossing the stream in boats or on rafts, or perhaps trying to wade across at treacherous fords, with accidents and drownings taking their natural toll from time to time. The safety of a bridge crossing would deprive the river of its accustomed tribute of human lives. Ancient legends make it clear people once believed that when a bridge was built a human sacrifice was necessary in order to appease the angry river gods.

To this day most of the construction workers who build our big bridges believe that "a bridge demands a life." By that, of course, they mean that someone will die in an accident before the bridge is completed.

2

The First Great Bridge-Builders

It is always interesting to remember that no matter how familiar and simple an idea may seem to us today, someone had to think of it first.

The first great architectural invention was the arch.

The false arch came first, and the reason it is called false is apparent. The central brick of the arch could be held in place with mortar, but it would not be able to bear much weight.

More than six thousand years ago people were building false arches. By 4000 B.C., perhaps by a happy accident, they had stumbled on the principle of the true arch.

We know this date because examples at least that old have been unearthed in Mesopotamia, in Asia Minor. While constructing an arch some builder must have turned his bricks on end, instead of laying them flat, and had the surprise of his life when he found they stayed in place!

The discovery must have occurred even earlier, because by 4000 B.C. the fully developed true arch, the "voussoir arch," was being built. A voussoir is a tapering or wedge-shaped brick or stone, and it is this wedge shape that makes the true arch work. The more weight placed on top

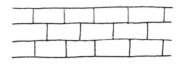

COURSE OF BRICKS

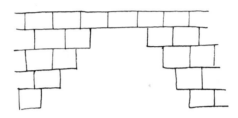

FALSE ARCH

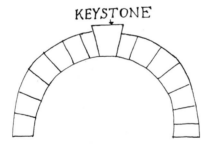

KEYSTONE

TRUE ARCH

of them, the harder the voussoirs press together. They will stay together without mortar; pressure keeps them in place.

Pressure always has to go somewhere, however. The arch thrusts the pressure of the weight it is bearing against the side walls that support it. If these side walls are not strong enough, they will spread apart, and then of course the arch will fall.

But now we come to an almost incredible fact. Even though the arch was thought of all those thousands of years ago it was used only in buildings, tombs, and under-ground vaults. During the next thirty-five hundred years nobody seems to have thought of using the arch to build bridges.

The people who thought of doing that were the greatest builders the world had ever seen, and the first people to build truly great and lasting bridges—the Romans.

The Romans were the first real engineers. They loved to build, especially on a grand scale, and they have left their walls, columns, temples, triumphal arches, tombs, baths, amphitheaters, bridges, and aqueducts all over their former empire, in Europe, Asia Minor, and North Africa. In some ways their bridges deserve to be called their greatest triumphs, because while most of the other struc-tures are ruins now, many of their bridges are still being used.

To be sure, the Romans did not start out by building bridges of stone or brick. At first they used wood, and relatively simple methods of construction.

Sometimes, when the water was shallow enough, they drove lines of pilings into a river bed and built their

10

bridge on top of the pilings. On one of his military expeditions Julius Caesar built such a bridge across the Rhine. The spans between pilings were 20 to 25 feet long, and the whole bridge was somewhere between 1300 and 1600 feet long. In only ten days' time his army had cut the timber, built the bridge, and crossed it! Later on, when the bridge had served its purpose, the same army destroyed it.

Sometimes the footing for a pier was built up simply by dumping slabs of stone into the water until the rubble piled up high enough and broad enough to support the foundation. The first Roman bridge we know about was the Pons Sublicius—"Bridge of Piles." It was built across the Tiber in the seventh century B.C., and one of the most famous of all bridge stories concerns it.

An army of the Etruscans was approaching Rome. The only way it could capture Rome was by crossing the Pons Sublicius. The Roman consuls decided the bridge must be destroyed. By then, however, the Etruscans were too close. There was not enough time, unless the enemy's crossing could be delayed.

Armed with sword and shield a brave warrior named Horatius Cocles rushed out onto the bridge to confront the entire Etruscan army—alone! At once two other brave men joined him, and the three of them held the bridge long enough for other Romans to destroy it behind them. No matter how large the Etruscan army was, only a few of its men could face the Romans on the narrow bridge at one time.

When the spans behind them were nearly destroyed, Horatius ordered his two comrades to retreat to safety. They had scarcely done so when the weakened spans collapsed. Then, wounded and still wearing his heavy armor, Horatius flung himself into the Tiber and swam for shore. Despite his wounds, his armor, and the spears that were thrown at him by the enemy, he made it to shore.

The Romans honored Horatius with a public statue and as much land as he could drive a plough around in one day. More than two thousand years later he was further honored by the English poet, Macaulay, who wrote a poem that every schoolboy in Victorian times knew, sometimes by heart—and it is 579 lines long! The poem, called "Horatius at the Bridge," ends with these lines:

> With weeping and with laughter
>   Still is the story told,
> How well Horatius kept the bridge
>   In the brave days of old.

The time came when temporary structures no longer satisfied the Romans, when they wanted permanent evidence of their grandeur. The stone-arch bridge was one result of this urge.

For bridges as heavy as these would be, the old ways of building up footings for the piers were not sufficient. What was needed now was to drive piles into the river bottom as far as they would go, then cut them off far below water level and top them with a heavy platform on which the foundation for the pier could be constructed.

Obviously it was impossible for people to accomplish such work underwater, and yet some way had to be found for them to work below the water level. The Romans solved this problem by building a cofferdam.

When it was decided where a pier was to be located, a

circle of piles was driven into the riverbed around the site, a circle perhaps fifty feet in diameter. Just inside this circle another circle was added, and the space between them was filled with clay. Once this was done, the bucket brigade went to work.

The Romans had plenty of cheap manpower to work with, because they had slaves by the thousands. As many slaves as were needed were put to work bailing the water out of the center of the cofferdam. It was hard and discouraging work. The clay in the sides of the dam was impervious to water, but water would often seep up into the cofferdam through the river bottom almost as fast as the men were able to bail it out at the top. Gradually, however, the water level was lowered enough to allow the engineers to set piles and drive them into the mud or sand or gravel at the bottom.

The Roman pile-driving machine consisted of a heavy stone which was lifted by a capstan wheel and dropped on the head of the pile. Engineers are happiest when their piles are driven to bedrock, but in many cases this is impractical. Wet sand, clay, or gravel under a riverbed will grip a pile firmly enough to enable it to bear tremendous loads without shifting.

A pile is driven to "refusal"—to the point at which further hammering fails to drive it any deeper. When all the piles for a pier foundation had been driven to refusal, the tops were cut off evenly a short distance above the river bottom and the spaces between them filled with stone and mortar. On top of this was built either a heavy timber platform or a concrete slab. The Romans had a wonderful mortar made of pozzolana, a volcanic clay, which was not affected by water. When this much of the foundation had been built, work began on the pier itself, which mounted layer by layer until it rose above the river and the masons no longer needed the cofferdam around them. The cofferdam was then removed.

Working in the mud and water of a river bottom was difficult and dangerous. People were often crushed or maimed by the pile driver or the piles. But the work on the foundations is the most important part of bridge-building. The part of a bridge that is underwater, the part we never see, is more important than the part we do see, because no matter how well made the superstructure may be, if the foundation is not solid the bridge will fall.

Not only did the pier foundations have to be solid, they also had to be protected as much as possible from wear. A flowing river constantly stirs up the bottom, so that the water's lower depths are a thick soup filled with mud and sand and pebbles which grind against anything in the path of the current. This action is called scour. To reduce the wear and tear of the current, the Romans built the fronts of their piers in the shape of a boat's prow.

The Romans used only one kind of arch, the semicircular. The arch describes a full half-circle from pier to pier. Each end of the half-circle rests on a pier, and the two piers will hold the arch up by themselves, even before the rest of the bridge is built, provided each pier is at least one third as thick as the width of the arch. Thus a bridge could be built one arch at a time, and if the work had to stop the partial structure would stay in place until work could be resumed. The Romans built their bridges during the summer and fall, when the weather was best and the water level was generally lowest, and stopped work during winter and spring.

14

The Roman arches were usually somewhere 50 and 90 feet wide, with the piers between 18 and 36 feet thick—a bit more than a third of the arch width, just to be on the safe side. Actually, the Romans did not have to make their piers as thick as they did, and of course narrower piers would have been an advantage, but the principles that made narrower piers safe were not known until long after the Roman Empire had passed into history.

Since the stretch of the Tiber that flows through Rome is 400 to 500 feet wide, it would take no fewer than five and as many as seven arches to span the river. Usually the number of arches was uneven, and the central arch was wider than the side arches. Putting the largest possible opening in the center of the stream was helpful to boat traffic, of course; but another reason for building bridges that way was that they looked better, and like bridge-builders almost everywhere, the Romans had soon begun to see beauty in the lines of a bridge.

Oddly enough the most beautiful of all surviving Roman bridges is not in Rome but in Rimini, a small city on the Adriatic coast of Italy. The Ponte di Augusto (*ponte* is the Italian word for bridge) is not a large bridge—of its five arches or spans the middle three are 28 feet wide and the end ones 23 feet—and its piers are unusual in that they are skewed slightly sideways rather than being at right angles to the current. It is decorated, however, in a particularly pleasing way, and faced with marble, and has been praised by artists and architects ever since it was built two thousand years ago.

The oldest Roman bridge in existence, dating from about 219 B.C., is also located outside of Rome itself, in this case in Spain. Nevertheless, the Eternal City remains in a class by itself, because six Roman bridges still have their feet planted in the Tiber there; and of those six five are still in use.

The sixth is called Ponte Rotto ("the broken bridge") because only one of its arches is still standing. The other bridges now carry cars, trucks, trolleys, buses, and hordes of pedestrians as sturdily as they once bore up under chariots and Roman legions.

Roman bridge roadways tended to be 25 to 30 feet wide, which means that the piers had to be that width, too. Work on an arch was started by erecting a timber frame

called falsework between two piers. This frame held up one row of voussoirs as they were set into place. The center stone is called the keystone. It is the last stone to be inserted in the arch, and locks all the others into place. When one semicircle of stones was completed the false-

ROMAN BRIDGE AT ALCANTARA

work was moved in order to support the next semicircle, and so on until the entire width of the arch under the roadway was filled in.

When bricks were used they were also wedge-shaped and were laid in overlapping courses as they would be in any other structure.

One reason the Romans built their bridges the way they did had to do with war. If an enemy managed to destroy one arch of a Roman bridge, the rest of it would still stand. The task of restoring the bridge, once the enemy had been driven off, was made much easier that way.

A type of Roman structure that should not be overlooked, even though it is not a bridge in the usual sense, is the aqueduct bridge, which carries water across valleys and rivers.

The Romans were the first to bring water supplies on a massive scale to their settlements. They had running water in their houses, in their fountains, and in their sewers. The most impressive surviving example of their aqueduct bridge is the Pont du Gard at Nîmes in France, built early in the first century A.D. when France was still part of Gaul and a Roman province.

Three tiers of arches march high across the valley above the river Gard, one atop the other. Six huge arches make up the bottom tier. The greatest of these clears the river in a span of eighty feet. The middle tier, stretching even farther in both directions, consists of eleven arches of similar size to those they stand upon. The top tier, which holds up the conduit through which the water runs, is made up of thirty-six smaller arches, each nearly sixteen feet wide.

Sometimes the Romans used mortar to hold blocks of stone together, and sometimes they clamped them together with iron bars. Here, for the two lower tiers, the stone-masons chipped and shaped and smoothed their blocks so carefully that neither mortar nor iron bars were needed. Only for the upper tier was mortar used.

The Pont du Gard is 885 feet long. The top tier is 155 feet above the river. The structure would be an impressive engineering feat even today.

Another kind of bridge the Romans built was used almost entirely for military purposes: the pontoon bridge.

Unlike the stone-arch bridge, the pontoon bridge was not a Roman invention, but had been built centuries earlier. The first one on record was built by a Persian king named Cyrus in 537 B.C. A pontoon is something, almost anything, that will float and support weight. Cyrus used stuffed animal skins. Lines of these were stretched

across the river and a roadway built on top of them.

Cyrus's successor, Darius, improved on this idea a few years later. In order to cross the Danube he ordered a bridge of boats to be built. Boats were anchored side by side from one bank of the river to the other and a bridge was laid on top of them.

Thirty years later another Persian king, Xerxes, built an even greater pontoon bridge across the Hellespont, with 360 ships in one row and 314 in another. The bridge was about a mile long. It took the Persian army, two million strong, seven days and seven nights to cross to the other side—where they lost the battle.

For over five hundred years Xerxes' pontoon bridge remained the longest ever built. Then a mad Roman emperor, Caligula, constructed a bridge of ships across the bays of Baia and Puteoli, about ninety miles south of Rome. Two rows of ships, with planking laid across to connect them, stretched for three and a half miles.

Caligula's bridge served no purpose whatever other than to show off his unlimited power. To show that he could walk on water as though it were dry land, he had the surface of his bridge covered with earth. Houses were even constructed on some of the ships for the convenience of the emperor and his followers, and fresh water was piped to them from shore.

His robes ablaze with jewels, Caligula led a procession across the bridge on horseback, followed by a great crowd of spectators who would have been wiser to stay home. Caligula was fond of demonstrating his power of life and death over his subjects. He did so then by ordering his soldiers to throw a great number of the common folk into the sea so that he could enjoy their drowning struggles.

A completely worthless bridge built by a cruel madman, then, held the record as the longest roadway bridge ever built for nearly nineteen centuries! Not until 1927 was it exceeded by a four and three-quarter-mile highway bridge across part of Lake Ponchartrain at New Orleans. Today the longest bridge in the world is the Lake Ponchartrain Causeway, 24 miles long, built in 1956. In 1969 a second bridge was built parallel to the first.

Caligula's bridge was certainly one of the few Roman bridges ever built without a practical purpose. But there is no denying that the Romans got practical things done by being cruel and ruthless. In a civilization built on slaves and soldiers, life was cheap. We may be sure that every bridge built involved many deaths. Nothing stopped the Romans from building, building, building. The peacetime occupation of the Roman soldiers tells a story in itself. When they were not fighting wars, they were put to work making bricks!

3

When London Bridge Was Built

When the Roman Empire finally crumbled, most of the
arts of civilization crumbled with it. They might have
been lost altogether had it not been for the men and
women who withdrew into monasteries and preserved as
much of the learning of the past as they could.

Whether the six centuries between 300 A.D. and 900 A.D.
deserve to be called the Dark Ages is a matter of opinion,
but certainly they were grim, troubled, and lawless times
for most people.

When times began to improve in the early Middle Ages
and people were ready to build again, it was the monks
who taught them how. A monastic order in northern Italy
became the Fratres Pontifices, the "Brotherhood of
Bridgebuilders," and took steps toward knitting together
the fabric of a civilization—knitting it with those indis-
pensable stitches called bridges.

Robbers, cutthroats, and highwaymen swarmed the
rough roads of that day and age. They were especially
dangerous at the points where travelers had to ford
rivers. Having all they could do to manage their horses
while crossing, travelers found it hard to defend themselves against attack. The monks began to build bridges

at such places. Inspired by the Fratres Pontifices, an order of French monks formed a similar organization and built a bridge on the river Durance near a ford that was so treacherous it was called *Maupas*—"bad step." Their bridge was so great a help to travelers that it was named *Bonpas*—"good step."

The new bridges were not built on the grand scale of the Roman bridges. Early ones were of the wooden-beam type, on stone piers or wooden piles. The men trained as workmen by the monks, the stonecutters, masons, plasterers, carpenters, and so on, were not slaves. They had to be paid for their work. The way of life that slowly came into being was vastly different from life in Roman times.

By the twelfth century, great days were once again dawning, and one of the earliest fine bridges of the Middle Ages came about in an amazing way—perhaps even miraculously, according to the story.

One day during a church service in the town of Avignon a young shepherd named Bénezèt suddenly interrupted the bishop's sermon to announce he had received a divine message: God had sent him to build a bridge across the Rhône!

The bishop thought the shepherd boy had lost his wits. To get rid of him he told Bénezèt he would believe him only if he could pick up a certain huge stone and carry it to the spot where God wished the bridge to be built.

Followed by the bishop and all the curious townsfolk the boy rushed out, prayed for a moment, then lifted the great weight and carried it easily to the riverbank.

The bishop knelt before him, calling the event a miracle, and his faithful flock immediately began to subscribe money for the bridge.

The bridge took ten years to build, and although the one-time shepherd boy died before it was completed, he was recognized as a bridge-builder and was canonized as Saint Bénezèt.

St. Bénezèt was further honored by having his bridge become his last resting place. A chapel was built on the bridge, and his tomb placed within it.

Today only four arches are still standing. No one knows for sure how many arches there were in all, but there were at least twenty. St. Bénezèt's bridge across the Rhône was actually three bridges. One, thought to have eight spans, led to an island in the middle of the river. Five more spans crossed the island. A third bridge, about the equal of the first, ran to the other side.

St. Bénezèt extended his piers with pointed cutwaters; and though he probably got the idea from Roman bridges he went the Romans one better by building cutwaters in both directions, an improvement that greatly reduced the whirlpool effect which otherwise resulted on the downstream side of piers.

He also improved on Roman designs in another way: he built handsomer arches. Probably by experimenting, since he did not know the scientific methods for planning curves, he worked out a pleasing curve that would also hold up safely.

Instead of being a full-centered curve, which would produce the semicircular arch the Romans used, it is a three-centered curve. Not only is it more satisfying to the eye, it also has the advantage of making possible wider openings between piers.

War and religion both had their effect on most medieval bridges in the form of chapels and fortifications.

25

Fortresslike towers guarded the bridges' approaches, while the roadway was narrowed at strategic points to make them easier to defend if an enemy force tried to cross. Horatius would have approved!

During this same period an English contemporary of St. Bénezèt was planning one of the most famous of all bridges—Old London Bridge.

Timber bridges spanning the Thames at London had been alternately constructed and destroyed ever since the tenth century. During one of their raids on England, Norsemen sailed up the Thames, made their lines fast to a bridge's pilings, then rowed downstream (helped by the current, no doubt) and pulled the bridge down. Another time they got around a bridge by digging a canal through the marshes south of London.

Toward the end of the twelfth century, however, when such invasions were no longer a threat and London was becoming an ever more important city, an ambitious builder named Peter Colechurch put forward his plans for a masonry arch bridge.

It was exactly what the medieval Londoners wanted. A fund drive was an immediate success, with subscriptions pouring in from rich and poor alike. For four centuries thereafter, the chapel on the bridge contained a list of the subscribers.

The old nursery rhyme we all know declares:

> London Bridge is falling down,
> Falling down,
> Falling down . . .

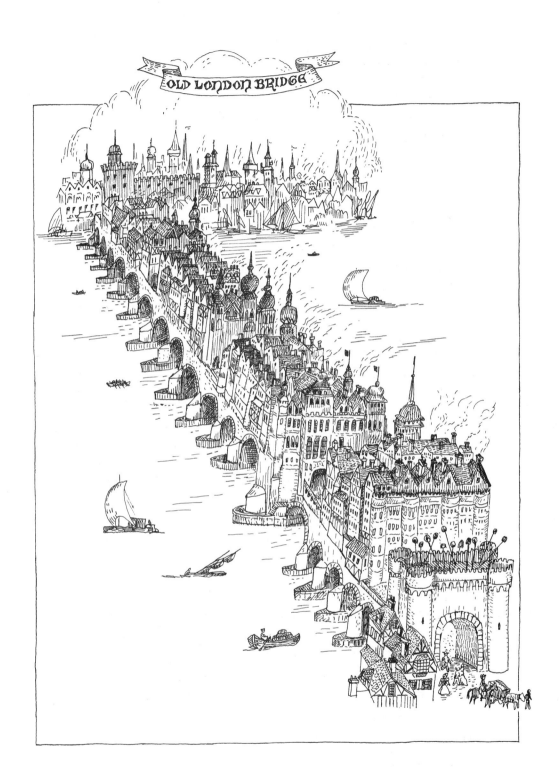

OLD LONDON BRIDGE

The amazing thing is that it *didn't!* It was a crude, clumsy-looking affair a bit over 936 feet long, with 19 pointed arches that varied in width all the way from 15 feet to 34 feet 5 inches. Not one of the piers matched any other, but all were more than half as wide as the arches that sprang from them.

This meant that the openings through which the waters of the tidal river rushed back and forth were relatively small. Water funneled through them with great velocity, making the passage of boats about as chancy as shooting the rapids in a mountain stream. In fact, maneuvering a boat through one of these arches was called "shooting the bridge," and a popular saying was that "London Bridge is made for wise men to go over and fools to go under."

In time about every structure one can think of was built on London Bridge. A gateway was built at each end and a chapel on the central pier; houses were added, built on corbels out over the piers, until there were a hundred of them, including buildings that straddled the roadway. In most of the buildings, merchants had shops on the roadway level and lived in the upper floors.

The seventh span from the south bank was a drawbridge. Upon the drawbridge pier, which was one of the larger piers, Nonesuch House was erected. It was called Nonesuch because nothing like it had been seen before.

We think of prefabricated houses as being a modern development, but Nonesuch House proves us wrong. It was a four-story prefabricated house brought over in pieces from Holland and fastened together with wooden pegs. In the first Queen Elizabeth's time it became one of the most fashionable addresses in London.

The south gateway was strongly fortified. Its defense

kept more than one rebellion from succeeding. When traitors were beheaded their heads were displayed on the battlements of this gateway, which soon gained the popular name of Traitor's Gate.

For most of its six hundred years London Bridge was the only bridge across the Thames. Its construction and upkeep—such as it was—were paid for by rents and tolls, and in time these amounted to a great deal of money. During some periods tolls were even collected for "shooting the bridge," which must have been especially galling to the boatmen who wished the structure had never been built in the first place.

Started in 1176, the bridge took thirty-four years to build. Like St. Bénezèt, Peter Colechurch did not live to see his bridge completed; and like the Frenchman, he was buried in his bridge's chapel.

By the seventeenth century Old London Bridge was no longer a fashionable address. Many of the houses fell into disrepair and were pulled down. Even so, the bridge endured almost to the time of Queen Victoria. In 1831 construction began on New London Bridge, and Old London Bridge was taken down. By that time several other bridges had been built at London.

Though few other bridges built in medieval times rivaled the Avignon and London bridges, the monks were responsible for many smaller ones that did them credit.

Arch curves became handsomer and of wider span, and the pointed arch appeared, as employed for Pont Valentré in Cahors, France, the finest medieval fortified bridge still in existence. Piers remained as wide or wider than ever, and for the same old reason—the dangers of war. To

Medieval Fortified Bridge

make sure each arch would stand independently should others in the bridge be destroyed, builders sometimes made their piers as much as two thirds the width of the arches.

Medieval builders imitated the earlier Roman methods of founding piers, but never progressed as far as learning the art of using cofferdams to make possible real construction below the water level. They had to use the easiest spots they could find, the shallows where the riverbed rose the highest or formed small islands, even if this meant an irregular spacing of piers with consequent uneven widths for the arches.

Piling up loose stones or driving piles to support a framework of heavy timbers provided foundations which often settled or shifted in the course of time. Because the piers were so large, the area which the scouring action of the river bottom could attack was all the greater, so that unless piers received constant attention and repair they were soon in a dangerous condition.

The Romans had two great advantages: their natural engineering skill which centuries of civilization had allowed to develop in an orderly fashion, and their enormous and cheap labor pool of slaves.

Nevertheless, because the people of the Middle Ages piled chapels, shops, towers, and battlements on their bridges, those structures became in some ways a more vital part of community life than bridges of earlier or later times.

4

Renaissance Bridges

As Europe moved toward the Renaissance, it entered an era that produced some of the most beautiful bridges of all time.

In Switzerland, a famous pair of covered bridges, mounted on timber piles, were built at Lucerne. They are important because they made partial use of the truss, an element of bridge construction which was beginning to be used without being thoroughly understood.

One of these, the Dance of Death Bridge, is also famous for the strange paintings that cover the underside of the roof. These pictures show all the stages of life, with Death always on hand in some corner of the scene.

A more cheerful covered bridge, built in the fourteenth century about the same time as the older of the two Swiss structures, is the Ponte Vecchio ("Old Bridge") in Florence, Italy.

There must have been little trouble in building piers in the Arno during the dry season. At that time the river is no more than knee-deep at the crossing point. One of Ponte Vecchio's remarkable features is its wide segmental arches, which vary from 90 to 100 feet in span. A segmental arch is a smaller arc of a larger circle than that

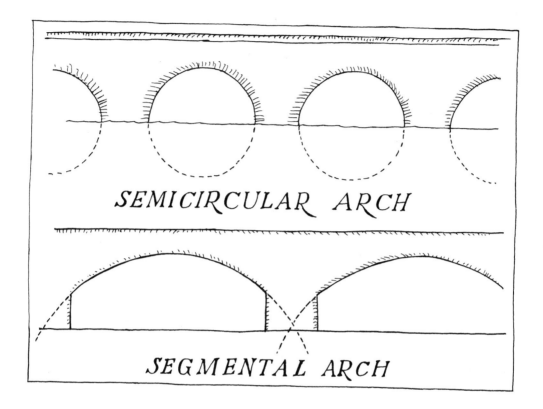

SEMICIRCULAR ARCH

SEGMENTAL ARCH

used for semicircular arches. The architect, Taddeo Gaddi, did not know how to figure out his arches mathematically, but he had a genius's sense of what would work. Despite several disastrous floods that tested it severely, his bridge has survived to this day.

Both sides of the Ponte Vecchio roadway are lined with jewelers' shops. Above them is a remarkable structure, known as Vasari's Gallery, which is a bridge on a bridge. A picture gallery itself, it connects two great palaces, now museums, that stand on opposite sides of the river.

Another bridge that was started at about this same time truly links the Middle Ages and the Renaissance—

because it took a century and a half to build. Built in Prague, the capital of Czechoslovakia, the Karlsbrucke was a formidable undertaking. The Moldau River was two thousand feet wide, with no convenient islands in the middle. When wars or religious conflicts or political problems were not holding up construction, a lack of money was. Not until 1503 was it finally completed.

Three years earlier, in 1500, work was begun on a bridge which established a record in the other direction. The first stone-arch bridge in Paris, the Pont Notre-Dame, was built to replace a timber bridge which had collapsed and caused several citizens to end their days in the River Seine. Thanks to King Louis XII, who knew how to get things moving, the Pont Notre-Dame was completed in the record time of seven years.

It was in the latter part of this same sixteenth century that perhaps the most famous and beloved covered bridge in Europe came into being: the Rialto in Venice.

Venice's canals are its city streets. Instead of cars and buses Venetians use a variety of boats, including the famous gondolas. The "Main Street" of Venice is called the Grand Canal. From the twelfth century on there was always one bridge across the Grand Canal at its narrowest point.

At first this was merely a wooden pontoon affair with a center drawspan that could be moved out of the way to allow boats to pass through. The Venetians made do with this, rebuilding it several times, until the middle of the thirteenth century, when a timber bridge on pilings was built. Because tolls were collected from all who crossed it, the new one was called the Money Bridge.

34

During the next two centuries and more, this too was rebuilt several times. When the Money Bridge was about one hundred years old a visiting celebrity caused a disaster. Remembering Caligula, it would seem an unhealthy pastime to gawk at emperors from bridges, though in this case the emperor Frederick III did not purposely cause the drownings. A huge crowd had gathered on the bridge to watch the pomp and pageantry of the emperor's arrival. Weakened by the jostling of such a mob, an iron railing gave way and many lives were lost.

Eventually a larger wooden bridge was built, lined with shops whose rent replaced the tolls, and built high enough in the center to allow boats without masts easy passage. To let masted vessels through there was a central span whose leaves could be raised like a drawbridge. Now that it was no longer a toll bridge its name was changed to that of the district it served, the Rialto.

THE RIALTO BRIDGE ACROSS THE GRAND CANAL

VENICE, ITALY

In 1512 a great fire swept through this district. While it raged there was a lot of talk about building a stone bridge to replace the old timber structure. But then the fire failed to reach the old bridge and that ended any prospects of change for another seventy-five years. It was 1587 before the Venetian senate finally went so far as to appoint a bridge committee. The winning set of plans was submitted by a distinguished old gentleman, Antonio da Ponte, whose surname means "bridge."

By now it was no longer necessary to allow for masted vessels, but a single arch was desirable in order to keep the entire width of the canal free for boat traffic. The segmental-arch curve gave a clear span of over 88 feet, with a rise of nearly 21 feet. The total width was over 75 feet. Two rows of shops line the central roadway. At first, as on Ponte Vecchio in Florence, the shops were occupied exclusively by jewelers.

By now people had again learned how to construct cofferdams and could drive, cut off, and cap pilings below water level. But da Ponte faced special difficulties. He had to work in soft, marshy ground close to large buildings on both banks. Abutments—the solid masses of rock or stone or masonry at either end of a bridge—normally take up considerable room. Because of the buildings, da Ponte had to build abutments that tilted outward. His enemies—disappointed architects who wanted the job themselves—stirred up trouble, claiming his foundations could not possibly be strong enough to hold up the planned single arch. A hearing was held, with the amusing result that the architect was saved by the sidewalk superintendants.

Then, as now, any large construction work attracted

people we call sidewalk superintendants today. These are the people who stand around watching for hours on end, fascinated by the work. In the case of da Ponte's bridge, these people knew from firsthand observation how thorough a job of pile-driving had been done. One man testified the pile-driving was so slowly and carefully done—in one instance taking three hours—that he had often fallen asleep watching. Da Ponte was given a vote of confidence, and work resumed.

The Rialto was finished after three and a half years. It is not a large bridge, but is one of the most beautiful and decorative ever built, and is notable for the skillful way it was fitted into a difficult setting.

The architect was then seventy-nine. Two years later he built another of the most famous covered bridges, the Bridge of Sighs, in Venice. This little gem connects the Ducal Palace and the prison, spanning the canal between them. When prisoners had been tried and sentenced in the Ducal Palace they were led directly to the prison across this bridge. The glimpse they had of the outside world through its grilled windows as they crossed was often the last they were ever to have; hence the melancholy name.

Two other bridges, not covered bridges, should be mentioned before we leave this great age in the history of bridge-building.

One of these would make most lists of the World's Ten Most Beautiful Bridges. Twenty-two years before the Rialto was finished in Venice, the Santa Trinità was built in Florence a few hundred yards downstream from Ponte Vecchio. The shallow curve of its arches has delighted, thrilled, and mystified bridge-lovers ever since. Whereas the rise of Roman arches equaled their span, the rise of most Renaissance arches was between one half and one quarter the width of the span. The rise of Santa Trinità's arches is only one seventh of their span!

During World War II a retreating German army blew up this beautiful structure. If you were to see it today, however, you would never know anything had happened to it. Restored perfectly, it was rebuilt for the most part with the very stones of the original.

A pair of statues flank the entrances on each side. They represent the Four Seasons. Summer, Autumn, and Winter were recovered almost intact, but Spring's head was missing. In 1961, however, even that final missing piece turned up on the waterfront, and local papers carried the headline, "Spring Has Returned!"

Toward the very end of the Renaissance still another of the world's best-known bridges came into being.

In Paris, the Pont Notre-Dame was nearly eighty years old and not in the best of health. Its foundations had settled, weakening it dangerously. A timber bridge, the Pont-au-Change, stood nearby, but was so crowded with moneylenders' stalls that it was unsafe for heavy traffic. A new bridge was ordered built, to be paid for by the national government. Its name became simply that—New Bridge, which in French is Pont Neuf.

Pont Neuf crossed an island which divided the Seine into two channels, one wide and one narrow. Thus the bridge had two arms, one long and one short.

Thanks to a variety of troubles, no building records were broken. Twenty-nine years passed before Pont Neuf was completed. Religious wars interrupted construction after one arm had been finished; and by the time work was resumed the foundations had been seriously damaged by scour, making extensive repairs necessary. Both the cofferdams and pile-driving of that period left much to be desired. Da Ponte must have driven his Rialto pilings pretty close to refusal, but in most places they never got that far. The result in too many cases was that foundations gradually shifted and settled.

Almost from the beginning, plans for the Pont Neuf included space for shops and houses. As with London Bridge, the Pont Neuf became a lively center of city life, where both high and low society were part of the passing show. Writes one historian, "The mountebanks, fortune-tellers, quack doctors, and tumblers, having established themselves there, attracted thither loafers, thieves, swindlers, pickpockets, and cutthroats."

From the beginning Pont Neuf played a part in Parisian history. Three years after the bridge was finished the king responsible for its completion, Henry IV, was assassinated. His was the first and last royal funeral procession to cross the bridge.

5

The Last Great Stone-Arch Bridges

Beginning in the late eighteenth century a new breed of men changed the face of the world by developing and using machinery. They were mechanics and engineers. John Rennie is an outstanding example of this new breed, because unlike most mechanics or engineers, he was both.

Though best known for his stone-arch bridges, he built iron bridges as well. He was a man born at exactly the right time to get the most out of his special talents.

His father was a Scottish farmer who died when John was five, leaving the boy's mother with nine children to care for. By then John was already displaying marked mechanical ability. He spent his playtime building miniature models.

Part of the family farmland was occupied by a tenant who was a millwright—a vitally important man in a grain-growing community. It was he who built the mills that ground flour, and kept them in repair. Tools and machinery were his stock-in-trade—and nothing in the world held more fascination for young John.

The mill shop was conveniently located on the way to the parish school. The millwright enjoyed the boy's interest in his work and gave him the run of the shop. As a result, many a day when the boy should have been in school he was building miniature ships, windmills, and waterwheels instead.

At the age of twelve Rennie talked his mother into letting him apprentice himself to the millwright. During the next two years he learned how to use tools, and studied the art and theory of mechanics. His occasional truancy from school had nothing to do with any lack of enthusiasm for learning. Throughout his life Rennie never stopped studying and learning.

Fortunately his family had a lot of good friends who recognized his unusual abilities and saw to it that they were developed. After two years with the millwright he was sent to a good high school where he plunged enthusiastically into the subject which would give him his most important tool of all and would turn a mechanic into an engineer: mathematics.

When he returned to the mill shop it was as an assistant, not an apprentice. Eventually he saved enough money to enter the University of Edinburgh. Each summer he worked again as a millwright to finance the next year at college. By the time he graduated he was trained in both the theory and practice of engineering.

A great opportunity came his way almost at once. James Watt needed an expert mechanic; Rennie applied. Watt, who had invented the first modern steam engine, was already famous. He was about to build the world's first steam-powered factory and needed the help of a man with more practical experience than himself. Rennie got the job, and the two men became lifelong friends.

During the next fifteen years Rennie was involved in a wide variety of engineering projects. The great work of his life, however, was bridge-building.

Rennie was twenty-four when he built his first bridge. It was small, as were many similar ones he built in the next few years. And all the time he continued to study, convinced that a designer should thoroughly understand the theories behind what he was doing as well as the practice.

One result of these studies was that Rennie had a world-wide knowledge of bridges. By 1809 several bridges kept Old London Bridge company in spanning the Thames, and another was being planned. Unsatisfied with the plans the designer had submitted, the company asked Rennie for his opinion.

He saw at once that the design was based on a famous French bridge built by a man who, during the first thirty-three years of Rennie's life, had been the world's greatest bridge-builder. His name was Perronet, and it was he who first grasped the principle that transformed the stone-arch bridge. This was that when a span was completely in place the thrust of the arches was not wholly downward; some of the thrust was transmitted horizontally all the way to the abutments.

Piers did not have to be as thick as the Romans had made them, nor even as had Renaissance builders. *One fifth* the width of the arches was enough to provide safety —even more safety than the thicker piers, because narrower piers provided that much less surface for scour to work on. The stone-arch bridge was perfected.

Like so many famous builders, Perronet died while building his masterpiece. At the ripe old age of eighty-six he died on the job in a construction shack on the site of his work-in-progress, the Pont de la Concorde.

The English designer's plan was based on Perronet's

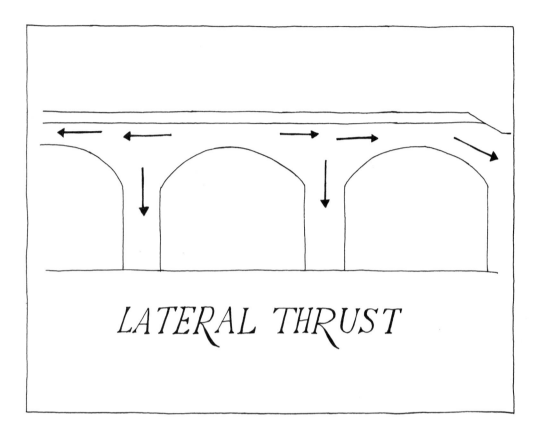

LATERAL THRUST

famous bridge at Neuilly, in France. Rennie knew that this bridge, however handsome it might be, had settled more than was good for it. So he criticized the plan for being based on a bridge that had serious foundation problems.

This was not altogether fair, since proper foundations this time would have corrected the defect. Nevertheless, the upshot of it all was fortunate. Asked to submit an alternative design, Rennie came up with one that would cost less, and he got the job. Instead of an imitation of a French bridge, Rennie gave London what many considered her most beautiful bridge—Waterloo Bridge.

For the next one hundred and twenty-one years this graceful stone-arch bridge, with its nine semielliptical arches, was sketched, painted, written about, and loved by several generations of artists, poets, and plain folk everywhere. When it was finally taken down in 1938, some people called it progress; others called it vandalism.

When the question of what to do about shaky Old London Bridge came up in the 1820s, however, it was no act of vandalism to suggest it was time for the bridge to go.

Asked for his opinion, Rennie made his usual thorough inspection of anything he was required to pass judgment

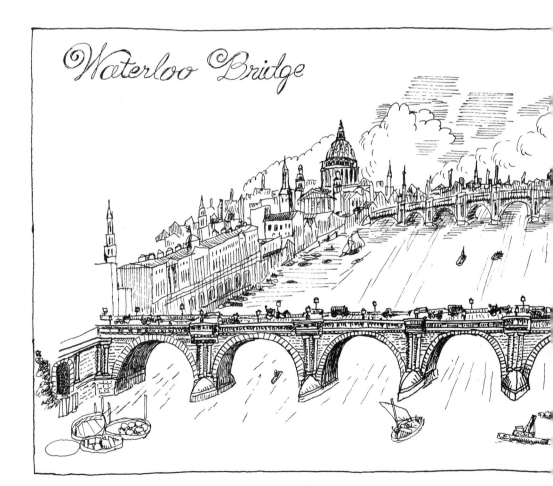

Waterloo Bridge

on and declared repairs impracticable. In his report he included a design for a new bridge. It was accepted.

Rennie was now sixty-one years old and in bad health. Like many another builder before his time and after he had trained his sons to follow in his footsteps. His son, Sir John Rennie, was his trusted assistant.

Many years before, the father had been offered knighthood by the king, but since he was only the son of a peasant farmer he thought this unfitting and refused the honor. In due time his son received the same offer and accepted—because he was the son of a distinguished engineer.

That he was worthy of the honor was shown by the way he carried out his father's great work. John Rennie died before work had begun on his New London Bridge, but Sir John saw it through.

The final fate of his great bridge would probably have amazed John Rennie as much as anyone. It settled into the Thames by about an eighth of an inch a year. This does not seem like much, but by 1968 it had settled a foot and a half and London authorities were alarmed. The bridge, they said, would have to be dismantled and either junked or sold.

Meanwhile, in Arizona, not far from the Grand Canyon, a new town was entering its fourth year of existence. It was a planned town built by a chain-saw manufacturer named McCullough, and lots were selling well; but something seemed to be missing. There was a big man-made lake with nice beaches nearby; but somehow the town itself had no focal point, no outstanding point of interest.

Then McCullough heard about London Bridge.

When the bridge was put up for sale, other promoters bid on it with the idea of merely cracking it up into souvenir-size pieces to sell in gift shops, carnivals, and fairs. McCullough topped them all with $2,400,000 and added another $1,000 for each of his 60 birthdays, making the grand total $2,460,000.

Taking the bridge down, shipping it stone by stone to Lake Havasu City, Arizona, and putting it up again added $5,600,000 to the cost for a super-grand total of $8,060,000. Originally it had taken a force of 800 men 7½ years to build New London Bridge. Forty men using modern equipment did the job in two years—but they did not have to found piers in the Thames.

The bridge paid off. Lake Havasu City has grown by leaps and bounds, attracting residents, businesses, and even factories. The English village along the embankment has been expanded to include a number of imitations of other aspects of the British Empire, past and present.

It hardly seems necessary to add that the plan for Lake Havasu City was drawn up by the man who designed Disneyland.

6

Bridges, Yankee Style

In stone bridges the arch is all-important. In truss bridges the vital form is the triangle.

If you nail four strips of wood together in a square or rectangle, with one nail at each corner, you can bend the figure out of shape. It will not hold anything up. Any weight on it, especially a moving weight, might cause it to collapse.

However, when you nail three pieces of wood together, you cannot change their basic form. A triangle cannot be distorted. This is what makes it such an important form in construction.

Prehistoric man learned to use the triangle as a frame for his roofs, and perhaps as a support for small bridges. A thousand years ago people built crude forms of the truss bridge, but without knowing how to give a truss the most strength.

Each length of wood that goes into making a truss is called a member. The long horizontal beams are called chords, or stringers. The vertical members are called uprights, or posts. The slanting members are called diagonals.

Two kinds of stress are involved in truss construction:

tension and compression. A member being pulled or stretched is under tension; a member bearing weight is under compression.

One of the basic spans uses the king-post principle. An upright divides the original triangle into two and greatly strengthens it. When the king post is above the roadway it is under tension, because the lower chord is pulling down on it. At the same time, the downward pull of the lower chord and the king post put the diagonals under compression. They are being squeezed together between the upper and lower chords.

Turn the span over, put the roadway on top of it, and the situation is reversed. Now the king-post is under compression and the diagonals are under tension. When the truss is above the roadway the structure is called a through truss. When the truss is below the roadway it is called a deck truss.

One way to lengthen a span is to use the queen-post construction. Here the top part of the large triangle is cut off, leaving two smaller right-angle triangles locking a square or rectangle into place between them.

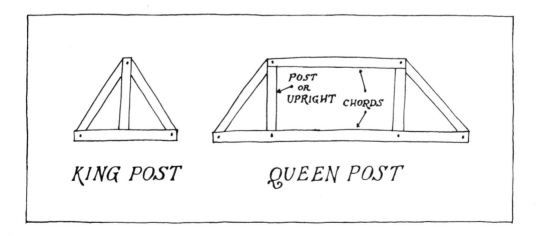

KING POST   QUEEN POST

The next step is a chain of triangles, called a multiple king post, and now we have arrived at a true truss.

In Switzerland and Germany diagonal members were used to strengthen wooden bridges long before the principles of tension and compression were completely understood. They were often bulkier and clumsier than they needed to be.

In the sixteenth century a great architect, Andrea Palladio, worked out the principles of four trusses and even built some truss bridges, but otherwise the form was disregarded and soon forgotten. Palladio lived and worked in Italy, where interest centered in stone and masonry. His great *Treatise on Architecture* was not translated and published in English until two centuries later, in 1742. It was in America that the wooden truss bridge finally came into wide use.

In places like New England the abundant supply of timber made wooden bridges inevitable.

Today a heavy snowfall leaves our bridges impassable until they have been ploughed. This was not the problem in those early days, because when it snowed almost everyone traveled in sleighs—in fact, tollgate keepers on covered bridges had to shovel a layer of snow *onto* their roadways so that sleighs could cross. But covering timber bridges had many advantages. The principal members were protected from the rot that resulted from too much moisture during rainy seasons, and from excessive drying under the hot summer sun. The covered bridge was not invented in America, but it achieved its finest flowering here. The more than one thousand still in existence have come to be looked on as a national treasure.

Many of the larger early bridges were not covered, how-
ever, including one of the most important. This was
Colonel Enoch Hale's bridge spanning the Connecticut
River at Bellows Falls, Vermont, built shortly after the
Revolutionary War.

Even though Bellows Falls was the river's narrowest
point, the bridge would still have to be over three hundred
feet long. While most people could see that a toll bridge
would be a money-maker there, few thought it could be
built.

Taking advantage of a midriver island Colonel Hale
planted his timber central pier there and came up with a
structure that made use of the cantilever principle. The
roadway, fifty feet above the water, was supported by
four sets of parallel braced stringers.

Only one workman was killed during the construction,
which was remarkable considering the ruggedness of the
site and the fact that no one involved had worked on a
bridge of that size before. Repaired only once during its
half century of use, it was finally replaced by a new toll
bridge.

Philadelphia was making do with a pontoon bridge—
on floating logs—across the Schuykill River. Timothy
Palmer was hired to erect a "permanent" structure.
With nearly 500 feet of river to cross Palmer planned a
three-arch bridge. To found his piers he used cofferdams
and set a new record by having to go more than 40 feet
below mean high water to found one of them. (Mean high
water is the average level reached at high tide by a body
of water affected by tides.)

Since the larger central span had a rise of two feet

more than the side spans the roadway was slightly arched. Including abutments the bridge was 1,300 feet long. The cornerstone, laid in 1800, bore this cryptic inscription:

TFCSOTSPBWL October xviii MDCCC

By the time General Lafayette made his triumphal return visit to America in 1824, the meaning of the letters had been forgotten by most people, but an old man was found who could decipher them for the distinguished visitor: "The First Corner Stone of the Schuykill Permanent Bridge Was Laid October eighteenth, 1800." Though by 1840 its name had become the Market Street Bridge, and though it was altered in 1850 to carry railway as well as carriage traffic, its "permanency" lasted till 1875, when it perished, as did so many wooden bridges, in a fire.

Meanwhile another builder, Theodore Burr, who may have read Palladio's treatises, or may have hit upon the idea on his own, worked out the design for a king-post truss, and for a while Burr-truss bridges were built all over New England. Burr strengthened his truss with an arch, which was a significant departure from the other builders' practice of strengthening arches with a truss.

It was Ithiel Town, however, who developed and patented a latticework truss that put bridge-building within the scope of every village carpenter. He advertised his bridge with the catchy claim that it could be "built by the mile and cut off by the yard," and so it could. His design was simple and economical, and it worked. Under his patent he collected a dollar a foot for every Town bridge built, and hundreds were.

But the days of large timber bridges were numbered. An important step in the development of the truss came when William Howe substituted wrought-iron verticals

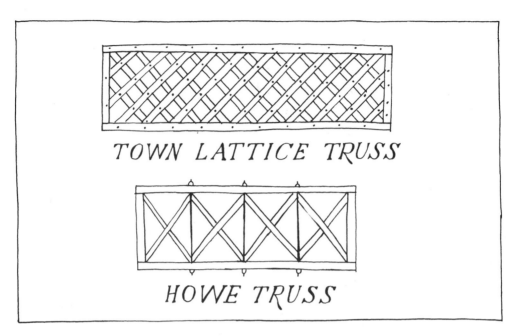

TOWN LATTICE TRUSS

HOWE TRUSS

for wooden ones in the truss he developed. For one thing, his verticals, made with screw ends to hold nuts and washers, could be mass-produced and shipped to local bridge-builders all over the country.

The truss bridge was used more extensively in America than anywhere else in the world; and it was here that the greatest advances were made in its design and construction, advances which were to continue when wooden-truss bridges yielded to iron, and iron to steel.

7

Iron Horses and Iron Bridges

The year after the American Revolution began, the first iron bridge was begun at Coalbrookdale in England.

At that time iron was still in the early stages of its development as a structural material. Coalbrookdale had become the world's first commercial center for the iron industry. Believing in their material, the local iron-masters seized the chance to demonstrate their metal's powers.

The 140-foot single-arch bridge was a success. Still standing, though no longer in use, it is preserved by the British government as a national monument.

New ideas, however, always win acceptance slowly. More than fifteen years went by before anyone even considered following the Coalbrookdale lead, and then it was an American revolutionary who did so—Tom Paine.

At Philadelphia, where Palmer's timber trussed-arch "permanent" bridge had not yet been built (the pontoon bridge was still in service), Paine planned an impressive iron arch of "three, four, or five hundred feet," in his own airy words. He got as far as having his arch ribs cast in England, but only one had been completed when his financial backing failed. By that time Paine had gone off to France, anyway, his attention irresistibly drawn to the French Revolution. It took another great Scottish bridge-builder, Thomas Telford, to show what really could be done with iron.

Like Rennie, Telford was born on a farm. He was an only child, rather than one of nine, but like Rennie's mother his was soon widowed. And like Rennie, he showed a great eagerness and aptitude for learning and received help from friends.

His first experience in bridge construction was stone-work, and was only one part of his general experience as a civil engineer. But his work happened to find him making his home in the heart of the iron-working country at the time the Coalbrookdale bridge was being planned and constructed.

He followed the project closely. He also gained intimate knowledge of Tom Paine's projected bridge. It was a long time before Telford's chance came—seventeen years after the Coalbrookdale bridge was finished—but finally in 1796 he designed and built the second iron-arch bridge only three miles from the first one.

This bridge, at Buildwas over the Severn, had a single 130-foot cast-iron span. Though it could accommodate more traffic than the earlier bridge its improved design used less than half as much iron. This made it much more economical than a stone-arch bridge of similar proportions.

To be sure, there was the usual lag between one form and another, the usual tendency to imitate the old form in the new. Iron has its own properties and does not need to conform to stone or brick patterns, but it took time for even Telford to recognize this. In Telford's as in the Coalbrookdale bridge, cast-iron blocks shaped as voussoirs made up the arches.

However, when Telford built his most beautiful iron bridge over a mountain stream in Scotland, its span consisted of two concentric arcs joined by diagonals—the first modern metal arch. He was learning.

Such achievements as these were important, of course, but they were not what made Telford famous. His greatest achievement was the Menai Strait Bridge—a true first, a suspension bridge of a size hitherto unknown.

Off the coast of Wales in the British Isles lies the island of Anglesea, separated from the mainland by the narrow and shallow Menai Strait. A span was badly needed, but no ordinary bridge would do. No piers could be founded in the channel, which had to be left absolutely clear for navigation—in fact, the bridge had to rise high enough to clear the masts of tall ships.

There were cliffs on both sides of the strait high enough to give a span 100 feet of clearance above the water, but the distance across was far greater than had ever yet been covered by a single span. Suspension bridges, with cables constructed of iron bars or links, were being built in increasing numbers both in the British Isles and America. Most involved spans of less than 100 feet. Telford's plan called for a main span of 580 feet!

The principle of the suspension bridge is simple. The cables are anchored in one abutment, carried to the top of the tower at that end, strung in an arc between the towers, and carried down to anchorage in the other abutment. The bridge's platform is supported by suspenders attached to the cables. On the tops of the towers the cables

MENAI STRAIGHT BRIDGE

ride on saddles which allow them to slip back and forth as the weight of the load being carried by the bridge changes.

It is a tribute to Telford's reputation that his plans were accepted by Parliament and the necessary funds voted. His most eminent colleagues, including John Rennie, had inspected his plans and backed them with their approval. In 1819 Telford went to work on the site.

Founding his two piers at water's edge presented relatively little difficulty. He had firm rock foundations to work with on both sides—above water on the west side and only six feet below water on the east. His most exacting task lay in making sure the tremendous iron chains would have the required strength.

Cast iron is iron which has been run in a molten state into molds where it has cooled or hardened. It stands up well under forces that press on it, but not those that pull on it, placing it under tension. By now, however, great improvements had been made in the properties of wrought iron, which is malleable and can be shaped or extended by beating with hammers or by pressure of rollers, and which now possessed great tensile strength. It was wrought iron that Telford tested and retested, making sure of each iron bar. Among the 935 bars that would make up the 16 cables there must not be one weak link.

Central portions of the chains were put together on rafts and floated out into position between the two piers. One end was attached to sections of chain hanging down from the tower of a pier. The other end was attached to ropes which ran up to the top of the opposite tower and down to huge capstans operated by 150 men.

Slowly the capstans hauled the great chains, one at a time, into place. Everything depended on this operation.

When the first chain had been successfully lifted into place a friend found Thomas Telford on his knees saying a prayer of thanksgiving, and ready to have his first good night's sleep in quite a while.

When it was finished, the bridge, including the iron arches which carried the roadway to the central span, was 1,710 feet long. After a century or so it was reconstructed to take care of the heavier traffic, but it is still a working bridge—and who would think such a modern-looking bridge was over 150 years old?

Motorcars use the bridge today. When it was built, however, it carried stagecoaches and wagons, and the days of the stagecoach were already numbered. The age of the railroad was beginning. The great new demand was for railroad bridges.

The man who designed the first railroad bridges was the same man who is often called the inventor of the railroad locomotive. His name was George Stephenson.

The term "inventor" is often loosely used. James Watt did not invent the steam engine. George Stephenson did not invent the railroad locomotive. But Watt *did* invent the first *efficient* steam engine, and Stephenson did invent the first efficient locomotive. And that, where inventions are concerned, is what counts.

Like Rennie and Telford, Stephenson came from a poor family, poorer even than theirs, since his did not have a farm to depend on. But like the other two, Stephenson had brains, talent, and intellectual curiosity. All three sought old-fashioned book-learning, and all three made their way with its help. Stephenson did not learn to read until he was eighteen—but learn he did, studying three

61

times a week at night school because he knew he would never know how to do the things he wanted to do unless he could read.

In 1829 Stephenson invented the Rocket, the locomotive that proved railroads were practicable. Since railroad tracks must remain very close to level, however, without much of an upgrade, a train cannot go far in most parts of the world without needing bridges. Out of necessity, George Stephenson became a bridge-builder.

Railroad bridges presented many special difficulties. They could not be placed at ideal points for each crossing; they had to be built on whatever ground lay along the line of the railway. Without iron, suitable bridges would have been hard to build without ruinous expenditure of time and money—but then, without iron the railroad would not have developed in the first place.

Stephenson's son Robert was a gifted engineer and his father's closest associate. Determined that his son should have the advantages he had lacked, George saw to it that Robert received a good education. When Robert brought his books home at night, the two studied them together.

By the time bridge construction was becoming an important activity for the Stephensons, the father was on the point of retiring. He was turning more and more of the firm's work over to Robert. Thus it was Robert who built one of the most remarkable of all railroad bridges. What is more, he built it within sight of Telford's great suspension bridge, across the Menai Strait.

Another problem presented by railroad bridges was that they had to carry far heavier loads than any in the past. Even the houses and chapels and towers of medieval bridges were not as weighty as a locomotive and a string of freight cars filled with heavy goods. Besides, the buildings were erected on the bridge piers; the trains moved across the entire bridge, testing each foot of it separately and successively.

And now Robert Stephenson was faced with the task of building a railroad bridge across the Menai Strait! How could it be done?

The Stephensons had built many short bridges with cast-iron beams long enough to support the structure from end to end. A huge iron bar would fill the bill— except that there was no way to make such an enormous bar or to handle it once it was made, besides which it would use up too much iron.

It is always worthwhile to imagine the impossible, however, and to consider it from all angles, because sometimes the impossible leads suddenly to the possible. All at once Stephenson found himself thinking . . . what if the huge iron bar was *hollow,* and the trains ran through it?

The result was four rectangular iron tubes, arranged in two pairs, stretching across the strait. There was a mid-channel rock upon which Stephenson could found a central pier. With this support, careful tests indicated, the bridge would stand without further bracing.

The long middle-span beams were assembled on land and floated out on pontoons to be positioned between the towers, after which hydraulic lifts raised them, fractions of an inch at a time, into place. High winds and powerful currents almost carried away the first of the tubes—even the onlookers who had assembled to watch the show had to lend a hand at the capstans that controlled the pon-

toons, to keep the whole rig from breaking loose. Like
Telford, Robert Stephenson lost a lot of sleep during his
struggles with the Menai Strait.

In 1850, however, he himself drove the last rivet into
the bridge and walked across it followed by three locomotives pulling cars that carried a thousand people. Un-

BRITANNIA BRIDGE

fortunately, the bridge was destroyed by vandals in 1973.

Not all railroad bridges were as successful as Stephenson's Britannia Bridge, however. There were still many things engineers did not understand about the stresses bridges might be exposed to. Along with their triumphs, railroad bridges were to have their full share of disasters.

"The Bridge Is Down!"

Ashtabula Creek, a modest little stream in Ohio, runs through a rugged gorge. In 1876 a railroad bridge crossed the gorge sixty-nine feet above the stream. It had been built eleven years earlier, in 1865, the year the Civil War ended. A modified Howe truss, it was a very special bridge, because unlike most railroad bridges in America at that time it was built entirely of iron.

A blizzard was raging on the night of December 29 when the Pacific Express started across at a cautious fifteen miles an hour. Snow lay in deep drifts everywhere.

The Pacific Express was a doubleheader—two locomotives were pulling its eleven cars. Halfway across the bridge Dan McGuire, the engineer of the lead locomotive, felt a sudden drag. He later said it felt as if he were "running uphill."

He slammed the throttle wide open; his engine lunged forward. Behind him he heard a grinding sound, then a rending crash. First his tender had sideswiped the abutment. Then the second locomotive had hit it head-on. As McGuire ground ahead, the coupling between his tender and the second locomotive parted, saving his life. McGuire's engine cleared the chasm just before the bridge broke up.

The rest of the train went thundering down in a jackstraw heap into the bottom of the gorge. The wood stoves used to heat the cars overturned and set them ablaze, burning to death many persons who had not already died in the crash. In all, ninety-two lives were lost that night or soon after. Of the forty-three passengers who survived, most must have been seriously injured. It was the worst train disaster to date in a nation where train disasters had been frequent.

America was a land of rickety bridges built by railroad companies more interested in profits than safety, or by shady contractors who cheated on the highway bridges they threw together. Though well-known builders were involved in the Ashtabula bridge, faulty design caused the collapse of the bridge. During the 1870s, one in every four eventually collapsed, an average of forty per year. In most cases there was loss of life, though not on the scale of the Ashtabula tragedy.

A major cause of railroad bridge wrecks was derailment. Especially in deep snow, train wheels were likely to slip off the rails. When that happened while a train was crossing a bridge, cars were slammed this way and that against the truss, setting up stresses the bridge could not withstand. In the case of the Ashtabula tragedy, the bridge collapsed and the collapse caused the derailment.

Poor construction and worse maintenance were the principal causes of bridge failure. One bridge went down under a load of empty coal cars! But since no one was killed the public remained unconcerned. Instead it looked for scapegoats after the major disasters, and in one case drove an innocent man, the chief engineer of the Pacific Express's line, to suicide.

Not all bridges of that period were badly built, of

•RAILROAD TRESTLE•

course. When builders came to realize that cast iron was
not strong enough even for compression members in railroad bridges, it was replaced by wrought iron. By mid-
century new truss designs had been developed by engineers with some scientific understanding of what they
were doing: the Whipple, Fink, and Bollman trusses.

Whipple wrote important books on the subject of
bridge-building, and his truss bridges stood the test of
time. Albert Fink's truss was favored in the newer,
western sections of the country, Bollman's in the east.
The first Bollman-truss bridge, with wrought-iron compression members and tie rods, was built in 1850 near
Harper's Ferry, West Virginia. The truss remained
standing for over eighty years, and was no longer in use
when an exceptionally violent spring flood finally carried
it away.

In the British Isles no such appalling record of failures
existed. There most construction seemed adequate. Nevertheless, it was in Scotland that the worst bridge disaster
of the nineteenth century took place, three years to the
day after the Ashtabula tragedy.

An estuary is an arm of the sea at the lower end of a
river, where a tidal river's mouth broadens out before
reaching the sea. Two great estuaries indent the eastern
coast of Scotland, the Firth of Forth and the Firth of
Tay. Both stood in the way of the development of railroad
lines.

Thomas Bouch was an eminent builder who was destined to be knighted, in tribute to his great success, a bare
six months before his career was smashed to bits. Not only
was he in charge of the design and construction of a great

bridge across the Firth of Tay, he was also busily engaged in drawing up plans for a huge bridge across the Firth of Forth. He confidently expected to build both of them.

When it was finished, the bridge that swept in a long curve across the Firth of Tay was considered one of the seven wonders of the modern world. The 85 wrought-iron truss spans were 200 to 285 feet long. The piers that supported them were cast-iron cylinders on a brick-and-stone masonry base.

In Britain trusses were called "girders." Except over the deep-water part of the firth the girders were below the railway tracks, supporting them. But for the section over deep water Bouch built thirteen girders above the tracks to provide more clearance for navigation.

Opened in 1877, for two years the bridge prospered. Later on, of course, incidents were recalled which should have been taken more seriously when they first occurred: during construction a couple of the thirteen high girders, as they were called, had been blown down by a sudden gale and had been replaced; some of the cast iron in the piers had been far from first-rate and had shown considerable deterioration after a year or so; locomotive engineers, eager to show up the ferries by overtaking them during a crossing, often drove their trains across the bridge at speeds far greater than regulations permitted. It is always easy to put together a list of particulars after the event.

Once again, as at Ashtabula, it was December 29. Behind the locomotive were six coaches filled with nearly a hundred passengers, and a brakeman's van (we would call it a caboose). A storm was raging, with a gale that had reached Force 12, hurricane strength, on the Beau-

71

Firth of Tay Bridge

fort scale: over 80 miles an hour, with gusts that went much higher.

In that terrible storm no one had a clear view of what happened. The signalman at the south end, who had sent his signal by wire across the bridge once the train had begun its crossing, saw nothing from his cabin alongside the approach. A friend who had joined him saw three flashes of light followed by one great flash. Only one thing was soon clear. The high girders had given way and plunged the entire train into the icy, storm-tossed waters

72

88 feet below. There were no eyewitness accounts, because not one of the train crew or passengers survived.

The disaster caused a worldwide sensation. In Scotland some of the more hidebound religious groups were quick to point out that this was unquestionably a judgment of the Lord on the godless railroads for running trains on the Sabbath—December 29, 1879, fell on a Sunday. But most of the British Isles took the view that the fault lay in the bridge's construction.

It was Sir Thomas Bouch's misfortune that he, like the rest of his contemporaries, had no real understanding of the science of aerodynamics—a science then scarcely born. The heaviest gusts of wind, hitting the High Girders broadside, had been too much for them.

To show how little was known about aerodynamics one needs only to mention the opinions of the Astronomer Royal, whose appropriate name was Sir George Airy. Bouch had consulted him about wind pressure. It was Airy's airy opinion that 10 pounds per square foot was the most wind pressure a bridge could possibly be subjected to.

After the Tay disaster Airy wrote a paper recommending an allowance of 120 pounds per square foot! British authorities ultimately settled on the more realistic figure of 56 pounds as a safety standard.

Sir Thomas had not done the solid, painstaking job the Rennies or Telford or the Stephensons would have done. Still, with better luck on the weather the Tay bridge might have stood for many more years. It was Bouch's bad luck that disaster overtook his work so soon.

There was now, of course, no question of his being allowed to build the Firth of Forth bridge. He was repeatedly subjected to exhausting and hostile questioning at the inquiries. When it was all over he went home and died soon afterward of a brief illness at the age of fifty-eight.

One positive thing his bridge *had* done, however, during its brief existence was to prove that a bridge across the Tay was a paying proposition. Work on a replacement was begun almost at once. Built a short distance upstream, it was another iron bridge much like the first, even to having 13 high girders spaced exactly alongside the piers that had supported the fallen girders. Each of the new high girders, however, was 2½ times as heavy as the old ones!

The "biggest bridge in the world," as it was then—the bridge over the Firth of Forth—is, in a way, a monstrous monument to the Tay disaster.

With Sir Thomas Bouch dead, the bridge was built by John Fowler and Benjamin Baker. They threw a cantilever bridge across the firth which, whatever else might be said about it, was designed to last.

In his book *Bridges and Their Builders,* David B. Steinman (himself one of America's greatest bridge-builders) described the Firth of Forth bridge in these words:

> A general view shows that the whole structure consists of two approach viaducts—one on either side—with the main cantilever structure itself over the water. The flooring, which carries a double railway track, runs at the same level throughout, 150 feet above the water. Beginning at the south end, there are four granite masonry

arches which end in the abutment for the south approach viaduct. Then the girder spans commence—ten in number; the end of the last one is supported in the south anchor pier. The north approach viaduct is composed of three similar arches, an abutment, and five similar girder spans. The bridge proper is comprised of two anchor arms flanking three huge main towers, from which cantilever arms project to carry the two suspended spans. Each main tower consists of four steel cylindrical columns which rest on separate circular masonry piers. The members of the anchor arms and cantilever arms are 675 feet long, and the suspended spans are 350 feet. The length of the bridge proper is 5,350 feet, and the total length, including the approaches, is 8,296 feet. Of the three towers, the two outer ones are exactly alike, but the third one, built on the central island of Inch-Garvie, is much heavier in construction. The foundation for each tower column is a circular granite pier, sunk by means of pneumatic caissons. The tower columns are battered, for increased stability against wind.

"Battered," in this sense, means that the sides of the towers slope inward.

If some timid soul were taken blindfolded to a good observation point near the bridge and then given a sudden close-up look at the thing, it might easily scare him to death. At first glance it seems impossible that anything on earth could be so big. It clomps across the Firth of Forth like a superdinosaur. Immense, massive, and faintly ridiculous, it is not the sort of bridge one can admire for its graceful lines.

It is, however, the greatest railroad bridge ever built—and the sort of bridge it is hard not to grow fond of.

Firth of Forth Bridge

Across the Niagara...

In mid-nineteenth-century America, as we have seen, some of the world's worst builders were at work. The record of bridge failures was unparalleled. Yet in those same years America was producing some of the greatest bridge-builders of all time.

The spectacular gorge below Niagara Falls presented a special challenge. The span would have to be 770 feet long and 240 feet in the air above the river. Only one kind was feasible—a suspension bridge.

Two American engineers, Charles Ellet and John A. Roebling, had already built impressive suspension bridges. Indeed, in 1849 Ellet completed what was then the longest one anywhere, a 1,010-foot span at Wheeling, West Virginia. The company chose him for the Niagara project.

Ellet was a colorful man, a brilliant daredevil with the instincts of a circus performer. His first problem was the same as the one that had faced the Peruvian Indians at the Apurimac River: how to get that first bit of line across the gorge.

This time the distance was beyond bow-and-arrow range. For Ellet, however, the problem merely provided a chance to have fun and get a lot of publicity into the bargain.

Five dollars to the first boy who could fly a kite across the gorge!

The boy who won the prize treasured the memory of his feat till his dying day more than eighty years later.

A kite string tied to a cord tied to a line tied to a rope tied to an iron-wire cable crossed the gorge, and once the cable was made fast Ellet himself became the first man ever to cross the gorge in midair. He pulled himself across in a basket carrier!

Within weeks a light service bridge, to be used during construction of the real bridge, was in place. On this platform—seven and one half feet wide, and without railings—Ellet now rode across the chasm on horseback.

The service bridge was his downfall, however, economically if not physically. Fitted with railings and opened to the public as a pedestrian toll bridge, it made so much money that Ellet and the company quarreled over how to split the profits. At one point the bridge company sent the local sheriff to take possession of the bridge. Ellet was ready for him—he had placed *cannons* on either end of the bridge. Finally, however, Ellet quit. Eventually Roebling took over.

The bridge John Roebling built was a two-level structure, with trains crossing on the top level and vehicles below. The two levels were joined by a heavy timber truss, making this the first suspension bridge with a true stiffening truss. Roebling was first to recognize the importance of stiffening in the form of a truss, or wire stays, or both, for suspension bridges, to minimize swaying or twisting. A year before the Niagara bridge was completed his beliefs were dramatically borne out by the collapse during a storm (fortunately with no loss of life) of Ellet's Wheeling bridge. Unlike Sir Thomas Bouch, Roebling had a sense of just how destructive violent windstorms might become. He responded to the Wheeling disaster by adding more stays to his Niagara bridge. It remained in service for forty-two years, by which time greatly increased loadings had rendered it obsolete.

In the meantime, on the banks of the Mississippi, the largest bridge the world had ever seen was about to be built by a man who had never before built a bridge of any kind.

Make no mistake about it, the Mississippi is the most powerful, dangerous, unpredictable, destructive river on the face of the earth.

For decades St. Louis had desperately needed a bridge across the Mississippi. Its rival to the north, the upstart city of Chicago, was threatening to outstrip St. Louis as a railroad center. In 1867, with the Civil War out of the way, rails were again moving westward and were only two years away from a coast-to-coast link.

But without a railroad bridge across the Mississippi St. Louis had little hope of any major share in that future. Ferrying trains across was a slow and tedious process, and during the worst stretches of winter it became impossible; then the huge ice fields which formed in the river simply cut off St. Louis entirely from the eastern part of the United States.

But how was anyone going to span a distance of over 1,500 feet, sinking piers into a muddy river which at the best of times was formidable and during springtime floods swept as much as 100,000 cubic feet of water per second past the levees at a speed of nearly nine miles an hour— 12½ feet per second? What could anyone do with a river whose level varied as much as 40 feet?

One man knew the river better than any other, probably better than any other man ever will. James Eads knew it from top to bottom, because for years he had made his living by going to the bottom to salvage wrecked steamboats.

In nineteenth-century America all forms of travel were dangerous, but steamboats were in a class by themselves. Snags ripped them open and sank them; explosions, fires, and groundings took their toll; hundreds of steamboats went to the bottom.

Eads found them, salvaged their cargoes, and even raised them when he could, whenever they were still more or less in one piece. Amazingly enough, after a thorough overhauling and a fresh coat of paint many a steamboat he raised took to the river again, as good as new.

During the Civil War Eads distinguished himself by building ironclad gunboats for the North. They shattered Confederate defenses along the Mississippi and materially affected the outcome of the war. (Our daredevil friend Charles Ellet was also active. He built a squadron of ironclad rams for use on the river. Naturally he led the attack on an enemy stronghold himself, and was mortally wounded during the victory.)

Once the war was over, the people of St. Louis could think about a bridge once again. Eads had never built one, had never even thought of building one, but now he was seized by the idea.

The bridge would have to be high enough to allow

steamboats with their tall smokestacks to pass beneath it, with the piers far enough apart to give them plenty of room for navigation. But most difficult of all would be the founding of the abutments on the banks and the piers out in the mighty stream. Given the awesome power of that current at floodtimes, and the ice jams that would pile up against the bridge in winter, there could be only one way to make sure the masonry would stand. It had to go to bedrock.

Eads possessed enough confidence to outfit ten ordinary men. Any man who had spent a lot of his life in a diving bell on the river bottom, groping in the mud for bars of pig iron and other valuable sunken cargo, *had* to have self-confidence. He also inspired confidence in others. With the country's leading builders to choose from, St. Louisans still favored their local man, a real river man, James Eads.

He had nearly finished his bridge by the time Bouch began building his across the Tay. Bouch complacently stuck to methods that had been used for a generation or so, without making a single advance or improvement in those methods. Meanwhile, Eads was making bridge history in at least three areas: materials, foundations, and superstructure construction.

First, the material. Iron was reaching its limits; a stronger material was needed. That material was now at hand, but had not yet been put to the test.

Steel was nothing new, of course. Men had known how to make steel for thousands of years—but not how to make it inexpensively. In England, Henry Bessemer found ways to do this and was knighted for his work; yet when Bouch was building his Tay bridge a few years earlier he could not have used steel in its construction even if he had possessed the vision to want to. Not until 1878 was steel officially approved in Great Britain as a structural material for bridges.

No such restrictions hampered Eads, however, and his studies of steel and experience with it led him to a great decision: he would use steel for the arch ribs of his bridge. It was the sort of decision which took monumental confidence to make—and stick with.

The problem of foundations brought about his second great innovation. He planned a steel-arch bridge with three spans of over five hundred feet each. This meant that, besides the abutments on the east and west banks, two piers would have to be built in the river. At first even Eads himself wondered if he could plant all his foundations on bedrock—and wondered how he could be certain his bridge would be safe if he didn't.

10

Across the Mississippi

The hard life James Eads had led on the river and in its muddy depths had taken its toll. His lungs were affected. In the fall of 1868 a bronchial ailment was severe enough to force him to go abroad, where he could regain his health in a warmer climate than that offered along the clammy, chilly banks of the upper Mississippi.

By that time the west abutment had been successfully built. Enormous difficulties were encountered because of a great mass of rubble, wrecks, and debris piled against the riverbank, including two wrecked steamboats, one piled on top of the other! But only a few feet below the bottom steamboat lay bedrock. Once Eads had found ingenious ways to cut through the junk pile and clear it away to make space for a cofferdam, the masonry of the abutment began steadily to mount.

But now his illness took Eads away, and without him on hand to run things work slowed almost to a standstill. All this must have seemed like a terrible misfortune to him and his associates. Yet because illness took him to France he had the opportunity to observe a new technique for underwater construction and come to the decision that well may have saved his bridge.

Eads already knew about the work being done abroad with pneumatic caissons, but thought they would be too risky in the Mississippi. Firsthand observation of French engineers' work changed his mind. He resolved to use these caissons even though he knew he would be going to depths far greater than those that had been reached in France.

To understand what a momentous step this was, we must first have a look at a pneumatic caisson.

Imagine an open-ended rectangular wooden box, sheathed in iron, as much as 82 feet tall and between 20 and 30 feet square. The bottom nine feet of the box is closed off from the upper part by a heavy timber roof. That lower, floorless section will be the air chamber.

All around the bottom edge of the box are triangular pieces of iron which will give the caisson its cutting edge as it sinks into the riverbed. Water will be kept out of the chamber by compressed air. The deeper the caisson goes, the more air pressure will be needed.

From inside the chamber workmen would dig deeper and deeper into the mud and rock and stone of the riverbed. Of course there had to be a way to remove this material, so an endless chain of buckets running up and down through a water lock would do the work. Meanwhile, on the heavy timber platform overhead, the masonry of the pier would be constructed. The ever-increasing weight of the masonry and the excavations of the workmen in the air chamber would cause the caisson to sink farther and farther into the riverbed until finally it rested on bedrock.

Workmen reached the chamber by way of a vertical

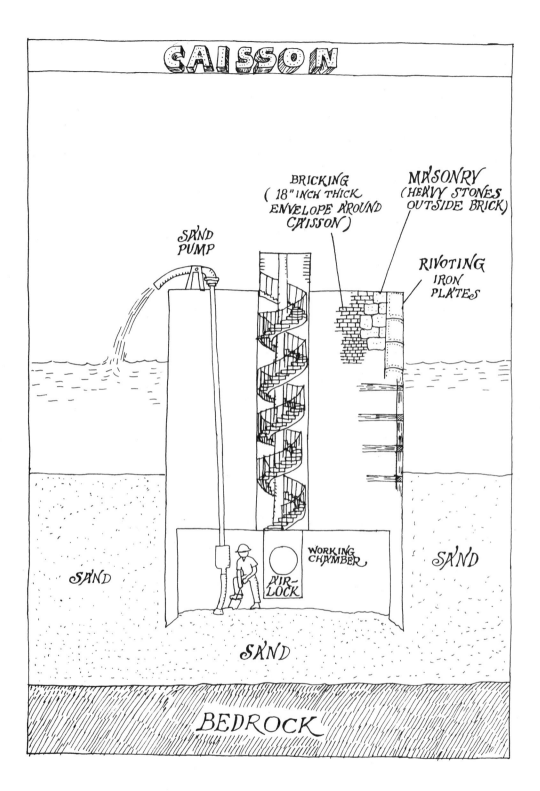

CAISSON

BRICKING
(18" INCH THICK
ENVELOPE AROUND
CAISSON)

MASONRY
(HEAVY STONES
OUTSIDE BRICK)

RIVOTING
IRON
PLATES

SAND
PUMP

WORKING
CHAMBER

AIR-
LOCK

SAND

SAND

SAND

BEDROCK

tube containing a spiral staircase, at the bottom of which was an air lock. Entering the air lock they closed the hatch, opened a valve, and let compressed air into the lock. When the pressure equaled that in the air chamber, they opened the door and entered the chamber.

Once bedrock was reached the chamber was filled with masonry, giving the final solid support to the pier that was rising above it. The upper masonry was built in the form of a hollow square, which would later be filled with concrete—including the tube down which the men had entered the chamber.

When the east pier caisson was towed into place in October, 1869, the river was about 14 feet deep. Below that, probes had shown, lay 81 feet of mud before bedrock would be reached.

Fifteen hundred men were used to man all the boats and barges needed to help get the enormous iron-clad box into position. Eighty-two feet tall, it rocked along on a great float which was removed once the caisson was squared away, with compressed air pumped into the chamber to keep it afloat.

At once work was begun on the masonry column to be erected on the timber roof of the chamber. Limestone blocks were lowered into the caisson. The column soon rose above the water level. It was important to keep the height well above water level in case the river suddenly started to rise. Within a few days the caisson rested on the river bottom. Now work in the air chamber could begin.

Atmospheric pressure at sea level is 14.7 pounds per square inch. At first not much more than this amount of pressure was found inside the chamber. As the caisson sank deeper, however, the pressure mounted. And with increased air compression came a new and frightening problem.

When the pressure had increased to nearly two atmospheres (14.7 x 2), trouble started. The workmen began to suffer from stomachaches and even moments of paralysis which, though only temporary, were frightening. Because their cramps caused men to double over in a sort of crouching position the disease was given its name—the bends.

It is easy to be wise after the fact. Today we wonder how engineers and doctors of those days could not have guessed at once that such sudden changes in atmospheric pressure could be dangerous and even lethal to human beings. Nature was generous in the hints she gave. The men did not suffer while they were working but only after they left the chamber. Many times men who were suffering mild attacks returned to work and, once in the chamber again, found almost instant relief from their miseries. These phenomena were reported, yet the significance of them never seemed to register—at least, not to the extent they should have.

The doctor Eads depended on finally ordered the men to stay in the air lock for several minutes when leaving the chamber. He was on the right track—but the rate was six times as fast as it should have been.

By the time the caisson reached bedrock, pressure was close to four atmospheres—44 pounds above normal. The men were allowed to work only six hours a day in three two-hour shifts, with two hours off between shifts. Cases of "caisson disease" became rare. Then one day a man who had come up from the chamber 15 minutes earlier in seemingly good condition suddenly fell over. In minutes he was dead. Despite all further precautions Eads and his doctor could think of taking, more deaths swiftly followed. In all, 12 men died, and others were crippled for life.

Many of the workmen were ill-clad and ill-nourished alcoholics. It was they who seemed most likely to suffer from the disease. Nevertheless, some of the precautions taken were effective. In the smaller west pier caisson, where the men never had to work under such great pressure, cases of the bends were few. The only man who died was one who did not bother to take the precautions ordered.

By the time the men had to go the deepest and work under the greatest pressure, in taking the east abutment to bedrock 136 feet below high-water mark, a lot had been learned or surmised. Instead of having to walk up, men were brought up from the chamber in an elevator. Only men in good physical condition were given jobs. They were examined daily and kept off the job if obviously unfit. At work, at least, they were well fed. As a result there were only four relatively mild cases of paralysis during the final foundation work, and the victims all soon recovered.

When the work was done, all four supports for the great bridge rested solidly on bedrock. Not even the might of the Mississippi could threaten them now.

The forging and assembly of the three majestic steel arches is another epic in itself. Only a man of Eads's exceptional character could have forced the steel manufacturers to keep to the high standards of production he

THE EADS BRIDGE OVER THE MISSISSIPPI

demanded. Every day brought new problems, and every day he found ways of meeting them.

The normal way to build the arches would have been the same way the Romans built their stone arches, by supporting them during construction with falsework. But falsework planted in the river between the piers and abutments would have impeded navigation. So Eads put the cantilever principle to work, building half an arch out in both directions from the piers, and half an arch from each of the abutments. In a sense, he built his falsework above instead of below.

Eads was like a juggler who had to keep half a dozen balls in the air at once. It would take all the space in this book to describe adequately the many problems he faced: the financing of the bridge; the opposition of other would-be builders who tried to undermine the public's faith in his work; opposition from the steamboat companies; and outrageous threats from the Secretary of War, William K. Bellknap, who would have had the half-finished bridge destroyed had not President Grant overruled him.

But always Eads seemed to find a solution for his problems—often because he had anticipated them. For example, when the time came to join the halves of the first completed arch Eads was in London trying to arrange for more financing. News that the arch had been successfully joined would make the additional financing a certainty. Back in St. Louis, however, there was trouble. The plan was to raise each half of the arch slightly by tightening the cables that held it up, then lower the halves together. But an unseasonable warm spell had hit St. Louis, and the halves had expanded just enough to make this method of closing impossible.

Eads had an alternate plan ready, another method of drawing the two halves together. It worked. The arch joined and held. The London banker came through with the money.

In 1874, seven years after Eads had first presented his plans for the bridge, its completion was honored with an all-out celebration by the citizens of St. Louis on the Fourth of July. A parade fifteen miles long crossed the bridge, with crowds watching from both banks and from scores of steamboats on the river.

The Eads Bridge—the first bridge to appear on a commemorative stamp, in the "Trans-Mississippi Issue" of 1898—is one of the few great bridges that have been named for their builders. Never was the honor better deserved.

11

Brooklyn Bridge

In July of 1867 James Eads presented his plans to the bridge company in St. Louis. Two months earlier, in New York City, John Roebling was appointed chief engineer of the Brooklyn Bridge project.

Eads was destined to build his bridge in seven years, to be present at the opening ceremonies, and to complete other great engineering projects.

Brooklyn Bridge took fourteen years to build, and neither John Roebling, who designed it, nor his son, Washington, who built it, was able to be present at the opening ceremonies.

Born in Germany, John Roebling received a good education and preparation for an engineering career. Neither the harsh Prussian government nor its rigid and unimaginative control of engineering projects were to his liking, however. It was illegal for any native workman to leave Prussia, but in 1831 he managed to get away. He came to America.

Within a few years he was working on a waterway with the wonderful name of the Sandy and Beaver Canal. In those days canals were still important. It was during this time that Roebling founded the family firm that is still doing business today. In certain situations flatboats were towed by hemp hawsers that frequently snapped, often killing people when they did. Roebling conceived the idea of using wire rope and began to manufacture it. It soon supplanted hemp.

His first construction was an aqueduct bridge designed to carry a canal over the Allegheny River. He built a suspension span. It was both successful and economical. While he was building the aqueduct, fire destroyed a nearby bridge. Roebling contracted to replace it with a suspension bridge, again with great success.

In time, besides spanning the Niagara Gorge, he built what was for a few years the world's greatest suspension bridge, with a span of 1,057 feet. The bridge crossed the Ohio River at Cincinnati. Work began in 1857 but was soon brought to a standstill, first by money problems and then by the Civil War. Cincinnati waited ten years to see its bridge completed.

A few months before the end of the war Washington Roebling left the Union army—with a citation and the rank of full colonel—to give his father some much-needed help in completing the Cincinnati bridge. He was then twenty-nine. Having seen active service on several bloody battlefields he probably thought his life's most dangerous period was behind him. If he did, he was wrong.

The ferry that ran between Brooklyn and Manhattan was famous in song and story, but as with the Mississippi at St. Louis there were times when the ice-clogged East River kept the ferryboats tied up for weeks on end. At such times the people on Long Island were, for all practical purposes, marooned. There had long been talk of building a bridge but nothing had come of it. The difficulties were obviously enormous, and the probable cost was frightening.

Roebling thought a suspension bridge was the answer. He said so as early as 1857, but it took another nine years for the financiers and politicians to work up enough nerve to get the project started.

The winter of 1866 helped matters by being the worst in the city's history. Ferry service was disrupted for long periods. By the time spring came the state legislature had approved the project and Roebling had been appointed chief engineer.

Needless to say there was opposition both from the public and from other engineers. A suspension bridge with an unheard-of span of nearly sixteen hundred feet? Preposterous! It took two more years to convince all interested parties that his plan was sound. In the summer of 1869 Congress finally passed the enabling act that cleared the way.

The East River was an important waterway for shipping. To avoid any possible obstruction of navigation the War Department set a requirement (which became the standard for all bridges over navigable waters) of 135 feet of clearance. Roebling's plans complied. They were complete in every detail. He was ready to go.

One week after he had received approval of his plans he was fatally injured. Ironically, the accident was caused by one of the carriers his bridge would make obsolete—a ferryboat.

He was standing on the Brooklyn wharf making a survey of the proposed location for one of his piers when a ferryboat entering the slip bumped against the side of it. Roebling's right foot was caught between the fender and the piles and crushed. In those days, before drugs such as penicillin were available, such accidents were often fatal. Within weeks tetanus had killed him. His son, who was his chief assistant, was left to finish the job.

Washington Roebling gave it everything he had.

The first important decision young Roebling made was to use pneumatic caissons. He went to St. Louis to see Eads's caissons. Later on they had a falling-out when Eads decided Roebling had helped himself too freely to ideas while inspecting the St. Louis caissons; but actually Roebling's were considerably different in design.

For one thing they were enormous—168 by 102 feet wide on the Brooklyn side, 172 by 102 on the New York side—and their air chamber was crosshatched with thick timber partitions that divided it into six working spaces each about 50 feet square. These partitions helped keep the huge caisson on an even keel as it sank into the river bottom. They also gave added support to the great pile of masonry that rose from the platform above.

The walls of the chamber, 9.5 feet high, were 9 feet thick at the top, where they met the timber roof. They tapered to the bottom of the chamber, and were shod in iron at the bottom to give them their cutting edge.

To make them watertight the insides of the caissons were treated in the same way as were the hulls of wooden sailing ships. They were calked with oakum which was coated with pitch. Several courses of timber covered the outside. Sheets of tin and planks treated with creosote were used to hold back both seawater and sea worms.

Because it would have to go deeper, and therefore support an even greater weight of masonry, the New York caisson's air chamber had a roof 22 feet thick rather than the 15 feet of the Brooklyn caisson.

On the Brooklyn side the greatest air pressure needed was 23 pounds per square inch above atmospheric pressure. Caisson disease was not a problem there, but lighting was. Electric lights were not yet in use, and illumination that involved smoke and flame spelled trouble. Oil lamps made too much smoke. Candles were better, but cost too much and burned too quickly in compressed air—a rich mixture in which any fire burns fiercely. Candles were also hard to put out; pinched off, the flame would reappear as if by magic.

Fires were frequent and stubbornly resisted all firefighting efforts. In the worst of these mishaps Roebling himself helped fight the fire for six hours. When the battle seemed to be won he collapsed and was brought out unconscious.

The fire had not surrendered, however, but had merely retreated. When Roebling had holes bored in the ceiling of the chamber the drill revealed a glowing mass of live coals deep in the timbers. To put the fire out once and for all it was necessary to flood the caisson. By now hundreds of tons of masonry were piled atop that fire-scarred flooring. Was it dangerously weakened? Would it give way and turn the half-constructed pier into a worthless block of tilted, off-center masonry?

Carefully the burned sections were cleaned out and filled with cement. In the end Roebling was able to say with confidence that the great platform was as strong or stronger than it had originally been. But the fire was only one of the many mishaps and tragedies that struck the bridge during its long years of construction. Worse yet, when the greater depths reached by the New York pier required 35 pounds above atmospheric pressure, cases of the bends began to appear with increasing severity.

The depth, 78 feet, was not much more than half the depth reached in constructing Eads's east abutment. Maximum pressure was nowhere nearly as great. Yet four times as many cases of the disease and three deaths occurred, because the doctor in charge did not know about the advances Eads's doctor had made in St. Louis. If the two engineers had been exchanging ideas, a great deal of human misery might have been prevented.

Worst of all, in 1872 Washington Roebling himself was struck down by the disease. Though he lived, he was an almost helpless paralytic during the years of work that followed.

Who, then, was to finish building the Brooklyn Bridge?

Washington Roebling. Though unable to walk, in constant pain, and unable to visit the site, he continued to supervise every phase of the work. From his apartment on Columbia Heights in Brooklyn he could survey the bridge through field glasses. He also had an invaluable asset: an extraordinary wife. Emily Roebling set to work and learned the business, including the necessary skills in mathematics and engineering, enough of both to make her his capable helper, his arms and legs.

The underwater work was almost finished. The great piers were soon completed, planted solidly on bedrock. Three more years went into the stupendous task of building the towers that were to support the cables, and the massive anchorage blocks that would hold them. Once that was done, the spinning of the cables could begin.

First came the wire ropes known as traveler ropes, because a "traveling wheel" would shuttle back and forth on them carrying the strands of wire that would eventually be bound together into cables. And those cables were not to be made of iron. For the first time, Roebling had long ago decided, this suspension bridge's cables were to be made of steel.

Each strand consisted of 286 wires. A hexagonal of six strands surrounded a single central strand. Twelve more strands surrounded this core to make one cable—a total of 5,434 steel wires, each as thick as a lead pencil, in each cable. Wires were laid parallel, then bound together.

Carrying a loop of wire the traveling wheel brought two lengths across the endless traveler ropes each trip. It cast the loop over a strand shoe, then returned empty while a second wheel was bringing two more lengths of wire.

Many people were still skeptical about the safety of long-span suspension bridges. Twenty-five years earlier a regiment marching in step had been crossing a bridge in Angers, France, when the bridge collapsed. Two hundred men were lost, the worst death toll in the history of bridge disasters. Nineteen years before that an American bridge had also given way under the feet of marching soldiers. After Angers, soldiers everywhere were ordered to break step when crossing a bridge. Yet in America several bridges had gone down under droves of cattle or flocks of sheep, which certainly were not marching in step. The truth was that the only reason for any of these failures was that the bridges were badly built or had become weakened owing to poor maintenance.

Though not concerned about the ability of his bridge to stand up under anything that might pass over it, Roebling was concerned about the force of the violent winds that often buffeted the East River. His father had stiffened his Niagara Gorge bridge with a lattice truss of heavy timbers and with inclined stays. The Brooklyn Bridge would have its steel trusses, and steel stays radiating down to the platform from the towers would add their stabilizing influence and strength.

In the design of the towers and the pattern created by the graceful stays Roebling created more than strength. He created beauty. Perhaps no bridge has ever been more often photographed from more different angles.

Roebling's triumph was complete—even though he could only watch from a distance, through his field glasses, as a glittering parade crossed the new bridge. President Chester A. Arthur and the governor of New York who would one day be president himself, Grover Cleveland, were both on hand for the event. Later in the evening a procession marched to Roebling's home led by President Arthur, who congratulated him personally.

Probably not more than a week or two passed, however, before some gullible country visitor to the big city became the first man to buy the Brooklyn Bridge from a smooth-talking confidence man. This transaction actually took place so often during the next few decades that it became a standard joke.

In case anyone has a romantic vision of Washington Roebling, his great work finished, lying back and expiring

THE OPENING OF THE BROOKLYN BRIDGE

after murmuring some suitable last words, here are the facts.

First of all, he partly recovered from his paralysis and was able to walk again. Twenty-one years after the bridge was finished, his wife died. Five years later, at the age of seventy-one, he married a second time. Thirteen years after that, when the deaths of his two brothers, no youngsters themselves, left the family firm without a head man, the eighty-four-year-old Washington was ready to go. Having no use for automobiles (even though by now his own firm was manufacturing a snappy car called the Mercer Raceabout), he went to work every day on the trolley car. He made quite a few changes in the plant while he was at it, bringing it up to date.

When he finished the Brooklyn Bridge, he was forty-five years old. When he died at the age of eighty-nine, the bridge was forty-four.

12

Twentieth-Century Bridges

With the twentieth century came a spectacular era of bridge-building. All previous records were broken. In periods of great progress, however, gaps in people's knowledge sometimes betray them. But we have to do and dare and, sometimes, learn the hard way.

In the first decade of the new century a huge cantilever bridge was being built across the St. Lawrence River at Quebec in Canada. Its 1,800-foot length was to outdo the gigantic Firth of Forth bridge by 100 feet.

The consulting engineer was Theodore Cooper. As a young man he had been one of Eads's assistants. One day during construction of the Eads Bridge he tripped on a plank and fell 90 feet into the river. He not only survived the fall but was back on the job as soon as he could change into dry clothes. He reported feeling a slight stiffness, but was otherwise fine.

Looking back, it must have seemed to him later as though life had spared him only for a much worse fate.

As was customary procedure for the cantilever method the anchor arms of the Quebec bridge were constructed first, supported by falsework. The cantilever arms and

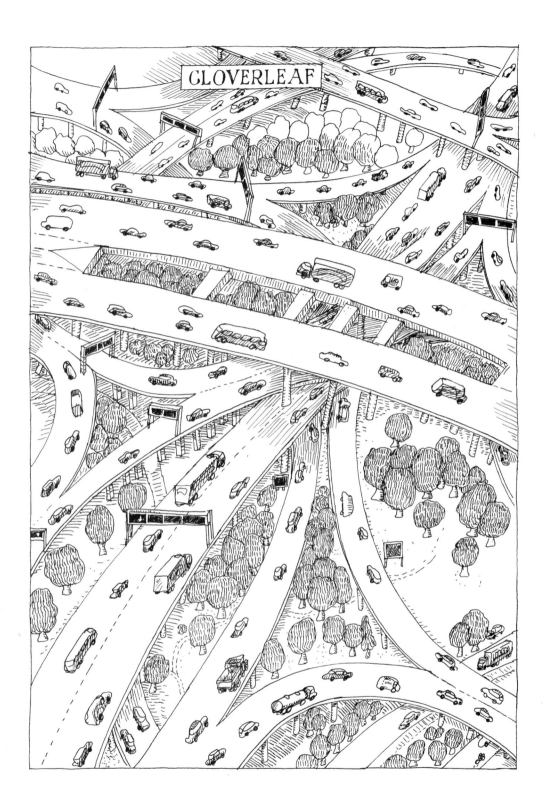

half of the suspended center span were then built out from each side. Cooper was in New York when word came from the engineers on the site that one of the nearly completed arms was bending down slightly. The deflection was only a fraction of an inch, but *any* deflection was alarming.

When he wired back to his engineers ordering an investigation Cooper made a fatal assumption. He assumed they would have sense enough to stop all work until after their investigation. They didn't. Nearly a hundred men were still at work on the bridge when the south arm and a third of the suspended span suddenly crumpled and plunged into the river. Eighty-two men were lost. Only eleven were saved.

The investigations and hearings lasted several years. When all was said and done the basic error was a familiar one: a lag in knowledge. Experience gained from smaller cantilever bridges, particularly in the design of compression members, had not been adequate when applied to the huge new bridge.

Nine years later, Quebec decided to try again. A new bridge was nearly finished when its center span was floated into position on barges—to be lifted into place this time.

Inch by inch the hydraulic jacks raised the span from the barges. It had been raised 12 feet when suddenly one of the hydraulic jacks broke. The 5,200-ton span went crashing into the river. This time eleven men died.

The following year another try was made. After four days of lifting the span was finally in place. And the Quebec Bridge is still the longest cantilever bridge ever built.

Ten years later two bridges were built across the Carquinez Strait in San Francisco Bay, the first of a great network of bridges there. In the next few years other long-span cantilevers were built at Montreal, Charleston, South Carolina, and across the Columbia River at Longview, Washington. A second one was built in San Francisco Bay, this time as part of the Bay Bridge—a series of approach spans, two suspension spans and a cantilever truss main span—which carries traffic across eight miles of the bay. Partway across the bridges reach rocky Yerba Buena Island. To take the roadway across the island a tunnel was bored through the rock, a tunnel which is bigger around inside than any other tunnel in the world.

The most spectacular strides, however, were now being made in suspension spans. For decades there had been talk of bridging the Hudson at New York City. In 1925 test borings were finally made at the proposed site, and an engineer named Othmar H. Ammann, with Cass Gilbert as consulting architect, began to build the George Washington Bridge—a bridge which *doubled* the length of any previously built span.

Despite the record height—600 feet—of the towers, the curve of the cables was far shallower than that of older bridges, because of the new bridge's great length, and the roadway was built without a stiffening truss. Significant advances in the tensile strength of steel wire made possible the suspension of greatly increased weight. Except for the Verrazzano-Narrows Bridge, built 35 years later by the same engineer, it is still the heaviest suspension bridge, much heavier than the longer Golden Gate Bridge. It was built for very heavy loads; nevertheless, it is one of the most handsome and graceful of bridges—and oddly enough, the touch that brings off the rare beauty of its design was not in the original plans.

Originally the towers were to be finished off with a covering of masonry. The steel framework of the towers was meant to be just that—a framework. But for once beauty and economics found themselves allies. Art lovers felt that masonry would spoil the beauty of the towers, and the builders saw a chance to economize. The towers were left as we see them today.

The success of the George Washington Bridge was a great help to the promoters of the Golden Gate Bridge. Before the first traffic had crossed the bridge in New York the San Francisco project had gone beyond the planning stage to the letting of contracts. At 4,200 feet, its suspension plan was 700 feet longer than the George Washington's. For the next three decades it held the record.

With growing confidence in their materials engineers were making their spans longer and longer in proportion to their widths, and the stiffening trusses smaller and smaller. Sooner or later, someone was bound to go too far.

On July 1, 1940, the Tacoma Narrows Bridge was opened to traffic across Puget Sound in the state of Washington. The third largest suspension span in the world, this bridge was seventy-two times as long as it was wide, and had no stiffening truss at all. Instead it had along its edges a solid plate girder only eight feet deep.

From the beginning, riding across the bridge was like riding a roller coaster. The bridge had a strange flexibility that quickly won it a nickname—Galloping Gertie. Far from frightening people away, however, its behavior drew record numbers of cars. Everybody wanted to experience the over-hill-and-dale effect of crossing Galloping Gertie. She was a big money-maker.

One morning early in November, when the bridge had been in service only a little over four months, during a gale Gertie began to do more than gallop. From a central point she began to twist in both directions, like a piece of ribbon candy. The bridge was cleared of all traffic. Onlookers gathered by the hundreds. The wind was slackening, but by then it was too late. First, sections of concrete slabs began to drop out of the center span. Finally a steel section fell, then more and more, until the entire center section went with a great crash into the Sound.

The death throes of the bridge, photographed by a university professor who had brought a movie camera to the scene, became a famous newsreel film. Only one life was lost when the bridge went down. When a newspaper reporter had to abandon his car on the bridge and run for his life, his pet dog refused to leave the car. Dog and car fell with the bridge.

Once again a bridge had gone down because not enough was understood about the forces exerted by wind—and scientists admit we are still far short of knowing all we should.

One hundred and fifty years ago a timber-arch bridge in Wettingen, Germany, had the longest single span of any bridge: 390 feet.

In 1826 Telford's Menai Strait suspension bridge exceeded it by nearly 200 feet.

For the next 63 years all successive record-holders were suspension bridges. Then a cantilever bridge, the Firth

Galloping Gertie

of Forth, reigned for 28 years until another cantilever, the Quebec, was finally finished on the third try.

But 10 years later, in 1929, the Quebec Bridge was outspanned by the Ambassador suspension bridge at Detroit, followed by the George Washington and Golden Gate. It seems unlikely that future titleholders will be anything other than suspension bridges.

The Golden Gate Bridge enjoyed 28 years of preeminence. The next "world's greatest," the Verrazzano-Narrows Bridge across the entrance to New York Harbor, is only 60 feet longer but in all other ways enormously larger and more costly. The four cables alone cost more than the entire Golden Gate Bridge. It may well be that at a total cost of $325,000,000 the Verrazzano-Narrows is the single most expensive structure of any kind ever built.

Its towers are so far apart that the curvature of the earth had to be taken into account in their construction. Because each tower stands exactly perpendicular to the earth's surface, they are $1\frac{5}{8}$ inches farther apart at their summits than at their bases.

Each cable is three feet thick, 7,205 feet long, and contains 26,108 pencil-thick steel wires. The wire in the four cables would reach more than halfway to the moon. Enough steel and concrete went into the bridge to build a town for 3,000 people.

Many of the construction workers were Indians from a tribe whose members have a special ability to work on bridges and skyscrapers without being bothered by heights. When the bridge "demanded its death," it was not one of them who fell. In the third year of the four it took to build the bridge, a worker slipped off the catwalk into space. Cooper survived a fall of 90 feet into the

Mississippi, but a man who falls 350 feet has no chance. A body hitting the water from that height might as well be hitting concrete.

By the time the Verrazzano-Narrows was built some techniques had changed. Men did not go down into pneumatic caissons to dig their way to bedrock. Now there was a vast rectangular honeycomb of cylindrical caissons. Huge derricks lowered clamshell buckets into them to dig out the pier foundations.

Some techniques had not changed, however. The traveling wheels, four feet in diameter, each weighing several hundred pounds, carried the wires across in the time honored way, and attached to each was a cowbell to warn workers of its approach—a cowbell like the ones that had been used since the first traveling wheel started rolling more than a century earlier.

New types of bridge construction are constantly being developed. In recent years one of the most important has been the box girder.

Box girders are hollow girders or beams with a square or rectangular cross section. They may be made of steel, or prestressed reinforced concrete, or posttensioned concrete. A spectacular example of box-girder construction is the Rio-Niteroi Bridge at Rio de Janeiro, Brazil.

The six-lane highway bridge, over eight miles long, includes a navigation span 984 feet long which rises 197 feet above the water. Since approach flight patterns to a city airport restricted the height of the bridge to 239 feet, towers were out of the question. Only a girder-type bridge was possible. Box girders were fabricated full size on

BOX GIRDER BRIDGE

land, floated out, and jacked up into position 197 feet above the water.

Many failures preceded the eventual success of the box girder. In the 1960s and early 1970s there were failures during construction in England, Australia, and West Germany. American bridge-builders have only recently begun to consider construction of box-girder bridges.

113

In Holland ingenious use of prefabricated steel-box girders made it possible to replace an old two-lane highway bridge with a new six-lane bridge with only a total of 10 days' closing of the bridge over the two-year period of the project.

Box-girder sections left the factory with asphalt surface, traffic lane lines, lighting, and guardrails already in place. A new section was floated 12 miles to the site of the 40-year-old bridge being replaced. Within 24 hours a

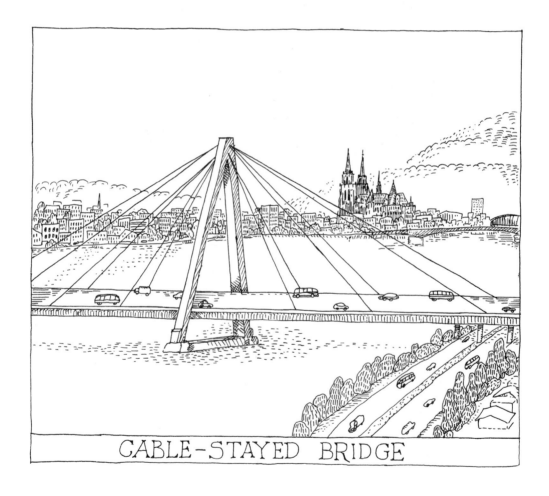

CABLE-STAYED BRIDGE

section of that bridge was removed from its piers and the new section took its place.

Cable-stayed bridges, another recent development, are modified cantilever bridges. Girders or trusses cantilever both ways from a central tower, and are supported by inclined cables attached to the tower at the top or sometimes at several levels—unlike suspension-bridge cables that are continuous from one abutment of the bridge to the other.

New possibilities are seldom overlooked for long. When a footbridge was needed in a remote area of Olympic National Park, a helicopter lifted laminated wood sections into place section by section.

At the same time the old ways have not been altogether forgotten. As part of our national observance a Bicentennial covered bridge was built by students of the University of Pennsylvania, members of the student chapter of the American Society of Civil Engineers. A composite of early Pennsylvania covered bridges, it was faithfully built in the old way, and used a Howe truss in its design.

13

The Infinite Variety of Bridges

Bridges have an infinite variety. Among the many kinds we have not touched on as yet are concrete; lift; rolling lift; swing; and the drawbridge or bascule.

Concrete as a building material was used for thousands of years, but it did not really come into its own until a Frenchman whose business was growing plants got an idea for making it stronger.

He needed big pots for big plants, and wanted to make them out of concrete. But to be strong enough the concrete had to be so thick and massive that the pots were too heavy to handle.

What if he started with a framework of iron wire netting in a mold and poured the concrete around it? Such was the beginning of reinforced concrete and its use as structural material. Today we find concrete bridges everywhere, and because of the plastic possibilities of reinforced concrete some of the bridges that have resulted are among the most beautiful of all.

The most notable lift bridge is still a railroad bridge across the Cape Cod Canal, though it was built many years ago. The span of such bridges can be lowered into

116

CAPE COD CANAL RAILROAD BRIDGE

place to allow trains to cross on a level, and raised high into the air to allow ships to pass underneath.

Rolling-lift bridges are built somewhat on the cantilever principle. The two leaves of the bridge meet in midstream. The onshore ends of these leaves are built into massive counterweights which help swing the leaves into the air when the bridge has to be opened.

Swing bridges work on the turntable principle, swinging sideways on a central pier, opening two clear channels through which ships can pass.

Drawbridges, of course, are familiar to everyone who has ever seen a movie or TV film complete with knights, castles, and moats. A body of water known as a moat surrounds the castle, with a drawbridge leading to the castle gate as the only means of crossing it. When the villainous Sir Roderick and his henchmen come riding across the moors to attack the castle, up comes the drawbridge.

In early times a huge stone, weighing nearly as much as the bridge itself, was used as a counterweight. With its help, the men inside the castle could raise the drawbridge by pulling on the ropes or chains attached to its outer edge.

For modern bascules the basic principle is still the same: a counterweight which makes it possible for small motors to furnish the modest amount of additional power needed to raise or lower the bridge.

But what about all the other bridges that surround us all over the world and are so much a part of life that too often we scarcely see them? What about wonderful little Chinese and Japanese bridges that arch like rainbows over small streams? What about bridges that run from building to building over city streets? What about the bridges that spring across our highways, sometimes with a quiet beauty or a functional grace that we don't even notice?

Just for the fun of it—just for the addition it makes to the joy of living—we should keep our eyes open when bridges are around. Once we have some idea of how they got there, and what went into building them, and what makes them good bridges if they are good or bad ones if they are ugly or badly built, it is surprising how interesting they become.

You may say to yourself, "Somebody ought to be able to build a better bridge than that—and I'm just the one to do it, once I've learned how!"

Index

Airy, Sir George, 73
Ambassador Bridge, 111
Ammann, Othmar H., 107
Angers, France, bridge disaster, 100
Ashtabula Bridge disaster, 66–67
Avignon bridge, 24–26

bascule bridges, 118
Bollman, Wendel, 70
Bouch, Sir Thomas, 70–74
box-girder bridges, 113–15
Bridge of Sighs, 37

Britannia Bridge, 62–65
Brooklyn Bridge, 94–103
Buildwas bridge, 56
Burr, Theodore, 53

cable-stayed bridges, 115
Caesar, Julius, 11
caissons, pneumatic, 85–89, 97–99
cantilever bridges, 6, 74–75, 104–106
Cape Cod Canal railroad bridge, 116
Carquinez Strait bridges, 107

Cincinnati bridge, 95
Coalbrookdale Bridge, 55
cofferdams, 12–14
Colechurch, Peter, 26–29
concrete bridges, 116
Cooper, Theodore, 104–106
covered bridges, 50

Dance of Death Bridge, 32
Da Ponte, Antonio, 36–37
drawbridges, 118

Eads Bridge, 80–93
Eads, James, 81–93, 97
Ellet, Charles, 78–79, 81

Fink, Albert, 70
Firth of Forth Bridge, 74–75
Firth of Tay Bridge disaster,
  70–74
Fratres Pontifices, 23

"Galloping Gertie" (Tacoma
  Narrows Bridge) disaster,
  108–109
George Washington Bridge,
  107–108
Gilbert, Cass, 107
Golden Gate Bridge, 107

Hale, Col. Enoch, 52
Horatius, 11
Howe, William, 53–54

Karlsbrucke (bridge), 34

Lake Ponchartrain Causeway,
  22

Menai Strait Bridge, 57–61

New London Bridge, 45–47
Niagara Bridge, 78–80

Old London Bridge, 26–29, 42

Paine, Tom, 55
Palladio, Andrea, 50
Palmer, Timothy, 52
Perronet, Jean Rodolphe, 42
Pons Sublicius, 11
Pont-au-Change, 38
Pont Neuf, 38–39
Pont Notre-Dame, 34, 38
Pont Valentré, 29
Ponte di Augusto, 15
Ponte Rotto, 16
Ponte Vecchio, 32
pontoon bridges, 20–22
prehistoric bridges, 2, 5

Quebec Bridge disaster, 104–106

Rennie, John, 40–45
Rennie, Sir John, 45–46
Rialto Bridge, 34–37
Rio-Niteroi Bridge, 112
Roebling, Emily, 99
Roebling, John A., 78–80, 94–97
Roebling, Washington, 95–103
rolling-lift bridges, 118

Saint Bénezèt, 24–25
San Francisco Bay Bridge, 107
Santa Trinità Bridge, 37–38
Schuykill Permanent Bridge,
  52–53
Stephenson, George, 61–62
Stephenson, Robert, 62–65
stone-arch bridges, 8–20, 25–47
suspension bridges, 3–4, 57–61,
  78–80, 94–103, 107–112
swing bridges, 118

Telford, Thomas, 56–61
Town, Ithiel, 53
truss bridges, 48–54, 66–74

Vasari's Gallery, 33
Verrazzano-Narrows Bridge,
    111–112

Waterloo Bridge, 43–44
Watt, James, 41, 61
Wheeling Bridge, 78, 80
Whipple, Squire, 70

DATE			
NOV 9	DEC 18		
NOV 30			
25			
OCT 6			
OCT 22			
DEC 18			
OCT 21			
NOV 11			
8 97			
NOV 22			
NOV 29			
JUN 0 ?			

© THE BAKER & TAYLOR CO.